W9-BXZ-586

Keep it Simple.   Make it Special.

Weeknight Dinners
6 Ingredients or Less

Dedication

For every cook that wants to create delicious and easy-to-make homemade dinners every night of the busy week.

Appreciation

Thanks to everyone who shared their simple and satisfying recipes with us!

Gooseberry Patch
An imprint of Globe Pequot
246 Goose Lane • Guilford, CT 06437

www.gooseberrypatch.com
1·800·854·6673

Table of Contents

Make-Ahead Monday Night Meals

(prepared and ready to go). 8

Busy-Night Burgers & Sandwiches

(with must-have sides) 40

Go-To Slow-Cooker Suppers

(sit back and relax). 74

Midweek Meatless Main Dishes

(quick vegetarian recipes) 110

Satisfying Salad Suppers

(served with tasty breads and crackers) 146

Pop-in-the-Oven Casseroles & Quiches

(all-in-one meals they'll love) 182

Stovetop Skillet Dinners

(simple and satisfying) 218

Mom's Best After-Dinner Desserts

(sweet delights). 248

Dinner-Friendly Snacks, Treats & Beverages

(goodies to munch and sip) 276

Weeknight Dinners Made Easy

Freezer-Friendly Make-Ahead Tips

In the first chapter of the book, we give you make-ahead recipes that you can have ready for the week or freeze for later. Here are some freezer-friendly tips that will help you enjoy dinner every night of the week!

▶ Spend a day making double batches of favorite foods to freeze. Your freezer will be full in no time.

▶ Cool down hot food before wrapping and freezing. Let just-baked casseroles stand at room temperature for 30 minutes. Then chill in the fridge for 30 minutes more. Large pots of simmering soup cool quickly when set in a sink full of ice water.

▶ Pack cooked foods in plastic freezer bags or food containers, or double-wrap tightly in plastic freezer wrap or aluminum foil.

▶ Label and date packages. When you reach for that package in the freezer you will know exactly when you made it.

▶ Most home-cooked foods are tastiest if kept frozen no longer than 2 to 3 months. As long as they're frozen solid, however, they don't become harmful to eat.

▶ Thaw frozen foods in the fridge overnight. If no baking instructions are given, cover casseroles loosely with aluminum foil and bake at 350 degrees for 25 minutes (for a 13"x9"pan). Uncover and bake 20 to 30 minutes longer or until hot in the center.

▶ When reheating thawed soups or sauces on the stovetop, make sure they are at a full boil for one minute.

▶ Many baked desserts such as cookies and cakes can be frozen in portion sizes and then thawed and served for quick sweet treats or snacks.

Have it on Hand

Keeping your pantry stocked with items that can complete your weeknight meal is easy to do and saves time. Here are some tips for having ingredients on hand to help you all week.

▶ Always keep canned fruits and vegetables in your pantry. Serving a quick can of fruit or veggies with a burger or casserole can make your meal complete.

▶ Keep loaves of purchased breads or flatbreads in your freezer for tasty additions to a soup or salad dinner. Bread freezes well and warms up easily in the microwave.

▶ Keep a variety of cheeses, both sliced and shredded, in your fridge to add as garnishes to burgers, soups, salads and other main dishes. Adding cheese makes the meal seem more complete and adds flavor and protein.

How we counted the 6 ingredients:

▶ **Salt and Pepper:** When the recipe indicates salt and pepper in the ingredients list, we did not count that as an ingredient. Each cook usually decides the amount of salt and pepper his or her family likes best.

▶ **Frostings:** The ingredients in the frosting recipes were not included in the 6 ingredients because the frosting may be added or omitted as desired.

▶ **Sauces and Dressings:** The ingredients in some of the dressings or sauces were not included in the 6 ingredients if the dressing or sauce could be used for other recipes or a purchased dressing or sauce could be substituted in the recipe.

▶ **Garnishes and Optional Ingredients:** These ingredients are not included in the 6 ingredients because they can be added or left out as desired.

U.S. to Metric Recipe Equivalents

Volume Measurements

1/4 teaspoon	1 mL
1/2 teaspoon	2 mL
1 teaspoon	5 mL
1 tablespoon = 3 teaspoons	15 mL
2 tablespoons = 1 fluid ounce	30 mL
1/4 cup	60 mL
1/3 cup	75 mL
1/2 cup = 4 fluid ounces	125 mL
1 cup = 8 fluid ounces	250 mL
2 cups = 1 pint = 16 fluid ounces	500 mL
4 cups = 1 quart	1 L

Weights

1 ounce	30 g
4 ounces	120 g
8 ounces	225 g
16 ounces = 1 pound	450 g

Oven Temperatures

300° F	150° C
325° F	160° C
350° F	180° C
375° F	190° C
400° F	200° C
450° F	230° C

Baking Pan Sizes

Square

8x8x2 inches	2 L = 20x20x5 cm
9x9x2 inches	2.5 L = 23x23x5 cm

Rectangular

13x9x2 inches	3.5 L = 33x23x5 cm

Loaf

9x5x3 inches	2 L = 23x13x7 cm

Round

8x1-1/2 inches	1.2 L = 20x4 cm
9x1-1/2 inches	1.5 L = 23x4 cm

Recipe Abbreviations

t. = teaspoon	ltr. = liter
T. = tablespoon	oz. = ounce
c. = cup	lb. = pound
pt. = pint	doz. = dozen
qt. = quart	pkg. = package
gal. = gallon	env. = envelope

Kitchen Measurements

A pinch = 1/8 tablespoon	1 fluid ounce = 2 tablespoons
3 teaspoons = 1 tablespoon	4 fluid ounces = 1/2 cup
2 tablespoons = 1/8 cup	8 fluid ounces = 1 cup
4 tablespoons = 1/4 cup	16 fluid ounces = 1 pint
8 tablespoons = 1/2 cup	32 fluid ounces = 1 quart
16 tablespoons = 1 cup	16 ounces net weight = 1 pound
2 cups = 1 pint	
4 cups = 1 quart	
4 quarts = 1 gallon	

Make-Ahead Monday Night Meals

(prepared and ready to go)

A busy week ahead? No worries! Get a jump start on meal prep with these tasty make-ahead recipes. Stir up a batch of Tasty Spaghetti Sauce with Quick Meatballs or some Muffin Tin Meatloaves to have in the freezer for just-in-time meals. Use your weekend time to make a Pepperoni & Cheese Quiche to bake and cut into individual portions to enjoy later in the week. Or prepare Jennifer's Soy Sauce Chicken the night before to bake the next day. Whatever recipes you choose, your weeknight dinner will be ready to go!

Garlic Parmesan Chicken

Charissa Lang, Bellevue, ID

This is my son's favorite. Instead of the boring fried chicken from the local deli, we can enjoy our own with one secret ingredient...sour cream!

1 sleeve round buttery crackers, crushed
1/2 c. grated Parmesan cheese
1 t. salt
1 t. garlic powder
4 boneless, skinless chicken breasts
1/2 c. sour cream
1/3 c. butter, melted

In a bowl, combine cracker crumbs, Parmesan cheese, salt and garlic powder. Pat chicken breasts dry. Using a pastry brush, coat both sides of each chicken breast in sour cream. Dredge chicken in cracker mixture. Place in a lightly greased 9"x9" baking pan. Drizzle melted butter over chicken. Bake, uncovered, at 350 degrees for 45 minutes, or until juices run clear and chicken is golden. Makes 4 servings.

Make-ahead directions: *Prepare recipe as directed but do not bake. Cover and refrigerate until ready to bake the next day, following baking instructions.*

Muffin Tin Meatloaves

Kathy Dean, Eau Claire, WI

These little gems cook up super fast, almost twice as fast as a traditional meatloaf.

1-1/2 lbs. lean ground beef
1 egg, lightly beaten
1 c. Italian-seasoned dry bread crumbs
1-1/2 c. zucchini, shredded
1/2 t. salt
1/4 c. catsup
Optional: dried parsley

In a large bowl, combine all ingredients except catsup and optional parsley. Mix lightly but thoroughly. Place 1/3 cup of beef mixture into each of 12 lightly greased muffin cups, pressing lightly. Spread catsup over tops. Sprinkle with dried parsley if desired. Bake at 400 degrees for 35 minutes, or until no pink remains and juices run clear. Makes 12 mini meatloaves.

Make-ahead directions: *Bake as directed; cool and freeze in freezer-safe containers. To serve, thaw in refrigerator for several hours to overnight. Bake at 350 degrees for a few minutes, until warmed through.*

Quick tip

Garden-fresh herbs are delicious. If you have them on hand, just use double the amount of dried herbs called for in a recipe.

Muffin Tin Meatloaves

Kristin's Perfect Pizza Dough

Kristin's Perfect Pizza Dough

Kristin Stone, Davis, CA

5 c. bread flour
1-1/2 t. salt
1 t. sugar
1-1/2 c. warm water
1-1/2 T. oil
1 env. quick-rising yeast
Garnish: favorite pizza toppings

In a bowl, combine flour, salt and sugar. Heat water until very warm, about 110 to 115 degrees. Add water to bowl along with oil and yeast; stir. Knead by hand for 3 minutes; form into a ball. Cover and let rise until double in size, about an hour. Punch down dough; let rest for 4 minutes. On a floured surface, roll out dough about 1/4-inch thick. Place on 2 ungreased 12" round pizza pans. Let rise an additional 10 to 15 minutes. Spread Pizza Sauce over dough; add desired toppings. Place in a cold oven; turn to 500 degrees. Bake for 17 to 20 minutes, until golden. Serves 6.

Make-ahead directions: Prepare dough as instructed but do not bake. Do not add Pizza Sauce or toppings. Cover and freeze dough on pans until ready to use. Add Pizza Sauce and toppings and bake when ready to serve. Will keep in freezer for up to 2 months.

Pizza Sauce:

8-oz. can tomato sauce
6-oz. can tomato paste
1-1/4 t. dried oregano
1-1/4 t. dried basil
1-1/4 t. garlic powder
1 t. salt

Stir together ingredients in a medium bowl. Spread onto Pizza Dough, add toppings and bake as directed.

Make-ahead directions: Make sauce as directed. Ladle into freezer container and freeze until ready to use. Will keep for up to 3 months.

My mom used to make this homemade pizza when I was a child and I adored it. Now that I'm an adult, I've perfected the no-cook sauce even more. You could also use the dough to make bread sticks...have fun with it! —Kristin

Salsa Lasagna

Lori Lybarger, Gambier, OH

Serve with sour cream and chopped green onions.

16-oz. can refried beans
1 c. salsa
9 lasagna noodles, cooked and divided
1 c. cottage cheese, divided
1-1/2 c. shredded Cheddar cheese, divided

Combine refried beans and salsa in a small saucepan; heat until warmed, stirring well. Spread 2 tablespoons of the salsa mixture in the bottom of an ungreased 8"x8" baking pan; arrange 3 noodles on top. Layer with half the remaining salsa mixture, half the cottage cheese and then 1/2 cup Cheddar cheese. Repeat layers beginning with the noodles; top with remaining noodles and Cheddar cheese. Bake at 350 degrees until bubbly, about 30 minutes. Makes 9 servings.

Make-ahead directions: *Prepare recipe as directed but do not bake. Cover and refrigerate until ready to bake the next day following baking instructions. Lasagna should be baked within 36 hours of preparation.*

Quick tip

Classic pesto is made with basil and pine nuts, but try other tasty combinations, like rosemary and pecans or oregano and almonds...delicious!

Fresh Herb Pesto Sauce

Fresh Herb Pesto Sauce

Colleen Hinker, Santa Rosa, NM

2 c. fresh herb leaves, coarsely chopped
6 cloves garlic, chopped
1 c. nuts, chopped
1/2 c. olive oil
1/2 t. salt
3/4 c. grated Parmesan or Romano cheese

Mix herbs, garlic, nuts, oil and salt in a blender. Process until smooth, adding a little more oil if needed to make blending easier. Transfer to a bowl and stir in grated cheese. Refrigerate in an airtight container. Makes about 1-1/2 cups.

Make-ahead directions: *Prepare as directed. Spoon into ice cube trays and freeze for later use in soups, salads, or casseroles.*

Grandmother's Red-Hot Salad

Tracee Cummins, Amarillo, TX

My great-grandmother was the perfect hostess. She always wore an apron and rarely sat down at family meals. Everything was always perfect at her table, from the sparkling china to the way the side dishes complemented the main course. She always served this salad at Easter alongside her beautiful baked ham...the spiciness of the salad is a perfect accompaniment to the mild flavor of the ham.

1/2 to 1 c. red cinnamon candies
1 c. boiling water
3-oz. pkg. cherry gelatin mix
1 c. applesauce

Add desired amount of candies to boiling water, depending on how spicy you want your salad to be. Stir until candies are melted; strain out any unmelted bits. Stir in dry gelatin mix until dissolved; add applesauce and mix well. Pour into a serving dish; chill until set. Serves 6.

Make-ahead directions: *Cover in refrigerator until ready to serve. Keeps in refrigerator for about 3 days.*

Jennifer's Soy Sauce Chicken

Susie Backus, Gooseberry Patch

12 to 18 chicken drumsticks
1/3 c. brown sugar, packed
1 t. dry mustard
15-oz. bottle soy sauce
1 t. garlic powder

Arrange drumsticks in a greased 13"x9" baking pan; set aside. Mix remaining ingredients in a bowl; pour over drumsticks and toss to coat. Cover and refrigerate 4 hours to overnight, turning chicken over once while marinating. Bake, uncovered, at 375 degrees for one hour and 15 minutes, or until chicken juices run clear when pierced. Serves 6 to 8.

Make-ahead directions: *Prepare recipe as directed but do not bake. Cover and refrigerate until ready to bake the next day following baking instructions. Chicken should be baked within 24 hours of preparation.*

This yummy recipe was shared with me by my good friend Jennifer. It's an easy make-ahead dish too, since it needs to be refrigerated at least four hours for the flavors to develop. Your family will love it! —Susie

Jennifer's Soy Sauce Chicken

Chili-Weather Chili

Mary Jo Babiarz, Spring Grove, IL

Serve with ciabitta bread and cheese for a complete meal.

1 lb. ground beef
2 T. onion, diced
15-3/4 oz. can chili beans with chili sauce
8-1/4 oz. can refried beans
8-oz. can tomato sauce
8-oz. jar salsa
Garnish: shredded cheese

Brown beef and onion together in a large stockpot; drain.
Add remaining ingredients. Bring to a boil and reduce
heat to medium; add 1/2 cup water if mixture is too thick.
Cover and simmer for 30 minutes, stirring occasionally.
Garnish with shredded cheese. Serves 4.

Make-ahead directions: *Prepare recipe as directed.
Refrigerate cooked recipe until ready to use. Heat
through before serving. Chili will keep in the refrigerator
for up to 4 days.*

Quick tip

Always have shredded cheese on hand for
topping soups or salads. A simple cheese
garnish adds color and flavor.

Chili-Weather Chili

Buffalo Chicken Pizza

Kris Coburn, Dansville, NY

Hot pepper sauce is available in several flavors and heat levels...choose one that's to your liking!

12-inch Italian pizza crust
1/4 c. butter, melted
1/4 c. hot pepper sauce
2 c. cooked chicken, diced
1/2 c. celery, chopped
4-oz. pkg. crumbled blue cheese

Place crust on a lightly greased 12" pizza pan; set aside. Combine butter and pepper sauce; mix well. Add chicken and celery, tossing to coat. Spread chicken mixture evenly over crust. Sprinkle with cheese. Bake at 450 degrees for 10 to 12 minutes, or until heated through and crust is crisp. Serves 4 to 6.

Make-ahead directions: *Prepare recipe but do not bake. Cover and freeze until ready to bake following recipe instructions. Frozen pizza will keep for up to 2 months.*

Mom's Meatloaf

Susan Biffignani, Fenton, MO

I make this often for friends feeling under the weather...it's always a hit.

2 to 3 lbs. ground beef
1 egg
10 to 12 saltine crackers, crushed
3/4 c. catsup, divided
1/4 c. onion, diced

Combine ground beef, egg, crackers, 1/4 cup catsup and onion together; pat into an ungreased 9"x5" loaf pan. Spread remaining catsup on top; bake at 350 degrees for one hour or until center is no longer pink. Makes 8 servings.

Make-ahead directions: *Bake as directed; cool, wrap and freeze in freezer-safe containers. To serve, thaw in refrigerator for several hours to overnight. Bake at 350 degrees for a few minutes, until warmed through.*

Buffalo Chicken Pizza

Baked Pork Medallions

Claire Bertram, Lexington, KY

My mother-in-law makes these fantastic medallions every New Year's Day. One more reason to celebrate!

1/2 c. grated Parmesan cheese
.6-oz. pkg. Italian salad dressing mix
1/4 c. red wine vinegar
2 T. olive oil
2 lbs. pork tenderloin, sliced into 1-inch-thick medallions
cooked fettuccine pasta
Garnish: chopped fresh chives

In a bowl, combine Parmesan cheese and salad dressing mix. In a separate bowl, whisk vinegar and oil. Dip medallions into vinegar mixture, then into Parmesan mixture. Place in an ungreased 13"x9" baking pan. Bake, uncovered, at 375 degrees for 30 to 35 minutes, until cooked through. Serve over pasta and garnish with chives. Serves 6 to 8.

Make-ahead directions: *Prepare recipe as directed except do not bake. Cover and refrigerate until the next day. Bake as directed.*

Grandma Dumeney's Baked Beans

Susan Fountain, Stanton, MI

My Grandma Dumeney brought her sweet baked beans to every family reunion...everyone really looked forward to them! Grandma was eighty-four when she shared this simple recipe with me, and I'm so glad she did!

3 28-oz. cans pork & beans
1 lb. bacon, crisply cooked and crumbled
1 c. brown sugar, packed
1 c. catsup
1 onion, diced

Combine all ingredients in a large bowl and mix well. Transfer to a lightly greased 4-quart casserole dish with a lid. Bake, covered, at 400 degrees for one hour. Reduce temperature to 350 degrees; uncover dish and bake for an additional hour. Serves 8.

Make-ahead directions: *Prepare as directed. Refrigerate until ready to bake the next day.*

Baked Pork Medallions

Grandma Dumeney's Baked Beans

5-Can Mexican Meal

Brenda Hughes, Houston, TX

In a hurry? I opened five cans from my pantry and made the best one-pot meal ever!

15-oz. can beef tamales, unwrapped and cut into
  1-inch pieces
16-oz. can light red kidney beans
16-oz. can pinto beans
11-oz. can sweet corn and diced peppers
10-oz. can diced tomatoes with green chiles

Combine all ingredients in a large saucepan without draining cans. Cook over medium heat, stirring occasionally, until hot and bubbly. Serves 6.

Make-ahead directions: *Prepare recipe but do not cook. Cover and refrigerate until the next day. Heat until hot and bubbly and serve.*

Tasty Spaghetti Sauce

Marilyn Morel, Keene, NH

My husband and boys love this tasty spaghetti sauce!

16-oz. pkg. spaghetti or other pasta, uncooked
1/4 c. onion, diced
2 t. canola oil
14-1/2 oz. can diced tomatoes
14-1/2 oz. can beef broth
garlic powder, salt and pepper to taste

Cook pasta according to package directions; drain. Meanwhile, in a large skillet over medium heat, cook onion in oil until tender. Stir in tomatoes, broth and seasonings. Bring to a boil. Reduce heat to low; cover and simmer for 10 minutes. Serve over pasta. Makes 4 servings.

Make-ahead directions: *Prepare recipe and freeze in freezer-safe containers. To serve, thaw in refrigerator; heat on stove until hot and bubbly.*

Quick Meatballs

Quick Meatballs

Carolyn Magyar, Ebensburg, PA

Make 'em ahead...they freeze well.

2 lbs. ground beef
1/4 lb. ground sausage
6-oz. pkg. beef-flavored stuffing mix
3 eggs, beaten

Mix all ingredients together; shape into one-inch balls. Arrange on an ungreased baking sheet; bake at 350 degrees for 30 to 45 minutes. Makes about 4 dozen.

Make-ahead directions: *Bake as directed; cool and freeze in freezer-safe containers. To serve, thaw in refrigerator for several hours to overnight. Bake at 350 degrees for a few minutes, until warmed through.*

Tasty Spaghetti Sauce
with Quick Meatballs

Homemade Soup Noodles

Patricia Tiede, Cheektowaga, NY

My mom always made these tender noodles for her chicken soup. She also served them tossed with butter as a hearty side dish. These can be made very quickly in your stand mixer with the dough hook. They're well worth the effort!

1-1/2 c. all-purpose flour
3/4 t. salt
3 large or 4 medium eggs, beaten

Combine all ingredients in a bowl; mix with a fork until dough forms. If too dry, add a few drops of water. Knead dough several times on a floured surface; roll out until very thin. Cut dough into thin strips or squares, as desired. Lay noodles on floured surface. Bring a large saucepan of water to a boil over high heat. Add noodles; boil about 15 minutes, until noodles rise to the top and puff up. Drain; add to hot soup or toss with butter and garnish as desired. Makes about 6 servings.

Make-ahead directions: Make noodles as instructed but do not boil. Let noodles dry for 4 to 5 hours until dry. Place in plastic bags and freeze until ready to use. Noodles will keep for up to 4 months in the freezer.

Homemade Soup Noodles

Tamara's Pickled Beets

Apricot-Glazed Ham Steaks

Kelly Alderson, Erie, PA

When it's grilling season, heat the ham over hot coals and serve with grilled apricot halves...oh-so-good!.

1/4 c. apricot preserves
1 T. mustard
1 t. lemon juice
1/8 t. cinnamon
4 ham steaks

In a small saucepan, combine all ingredients except ham. Cook and stir over low heat for 2 to 3 minutes. Place ham in a lightly greased 13"x9" baking pan. Pour sauce over ham. Bake, uncovered, at 350 degrees for 15 minutes, or until heated through. Serve ham topped with sauce from the pan. Makes 4 servings.

Make-ahead directions: *Prepare recipe as directed but do not bake. Cover and refrigerate. Uncover and bake as directed the next day.*

Tamara's Pickled Beets

Tamara Aherns, Sparta, MI

1/3 c. sugar
1/3 c. red wine vinegar
1/3 c. water
1/2 t. cinnamon
1/4 t. salt
1/4 t. ground cloves
5 whole peppercorns
2 c. red or golden beets, peeled, cooked and sliced, or
   16-oz. can sliced beets, drained

Combine all ingredients except beets in a saucepan over medium-high heat. Bring to a boil, stirring constantly. Add beets and return to a boil. Reduce heat and simmer, covered, 5 minutes. Let cool and chill for 4 hours to overnight before serving. Store in refrigerator. Serves 4 to 6.

Make-ahead directions: *Prepare as directed. Will keep in refrigerator for up to 2 weeks.*

Grandma knew how to keep fresh beets from staining her hands while cutting them. She rubbed her hands with vegetable oil first. —Tamara

Mom's Spaghetti & Meatballs

Elaine Lucas, Runge, TX

This started out as my mom's recipe. I've since made it my own over the years, and it's become a family favorite.

2 8-oz. cans tomato sauce
1/2 t. garlic powder
1/2 t. dried oregano
1/2 t. dried basil
16-oz. pkg. spaghetti, cooked

In a large skillet over medium-low heat, combine tomato sauce and seasonings. Bring to a simmer. Meanwhile, make Meatballs. Add uncooked meatballs to sauce. Simmer over medium-low heat for about 30 minutes, turning occasionally, until meatballs are no longer pink in the center. Serve sauce and meatballs over spaghetti. Serves 4 to 6.

Meatballs:

1 lb. lean ground beef
1/2 c. shredded Cheddar cheese
2 eggs, beaten
1 slice white bread, crumbled
1/2 t. garlic salt

Combine all ingredients in a large bowl; mix well. Form into 2-inch balls.

Make-ahead directions: *Prepare sauce and meatballs as directed. Ladle into freezer-safe containers and freeze. Thaw in refrigerator and heat when ready to use. Will keep up to 2 months in the freezer.*

Stuffed Pepper Soup

Charlotte Smith, Alexandria, PA

This is a great soup for a chilly day! It's so comforting and delicious. A good way to use some leftover cooked rice too.

1 lb. ground beef
1/2 c. onion, diced
28-oz. can diced tomatoes
1 green pepper, diced
14-oz. can beef broth
2 c. cooked rice
salt and pepper to taste
Garnish: chopped green onions

In a stockpot over medium heat, brown beef with onion; drain. Add tomatoes with juice and remaining ingredients. Reduce heat to medium-low. Simmer until green pepper is tender, about 30 minutes. Garnish with green onions. Makes 6 servings.

Make-ahead directions: *Prepare as directed. Cover and refrigerate until ready to serve the next day. Heat through before serving.*

Quick tip

Garnish soups and stews with fresh herbs, toasty croutons, or freshly grated cheese. Make your own croutons by cubing bread and frying in a little bit of butter. Yum!

Stuffed Pepper Soup

Make-Ahead Faux Lasagna

Make-Ahead Faux Lasagna

Juanita Lint, Forest Grove, OR

16-oz. pkg. wide egg noodles, uncooked
8-oz. pkg. cream cheese, softened
1-1/2 c. cottage cheese
1 lb. ground beef
1 T. dried, minced onion
8-oz. can tomato sauce
salt and pepper to taste

Boil half the package of noodles for 5 minutes; drain. Reserve remaining uncooked noodles for another use. Arrange half the cooked noodles in a lightly greased 2-quart casserole dish. Combine cheeses in a medium bowl. Spoon cheese mixture over noodles. Arrange remaining noodles on top; set aside. Brown beef and onion in a skillet over medium heat; drain well. Combine with tomato sauce, salt and pepper; spoon over noodles. Cover and refrigerate for one to 8 hours. Uncover and bake at 350 degrees for 30 minutes. Cover with aluminum foil and bake for 15 more minutes. Serves 10 to 12.

Make-ahead directions: *Prepare recipe as directed except do not bake. Cover and refrigerate until the next day. Bake as directed.*

This recipe came from a 1980 North Dakota church cookbook. It is a big hit...as tasty as lasagna but without the effort. That's how the name came about! —Juanita

Tom's Easy Meatloaf

Kelly Hargis, Essex, MD

2 to 3 lbs. ground beef
2 10-3/4 oz. cans French onion soup
6-oz. pkg. stuffing mix
2 eggs, beaten

In a large bowl, mix together all ingredients well. Form into 2 loaves; place in 2 lightly greased 13"x9" baking pans. Bake, uncovered, at 350 degrees for 1-1/2 hours. Makes 8 to 10 servings.

Make-ahead directions: *Prepare as directed but do not bake. Cover and freeze until ready to use. Thaw in refrigerator and bake as instructed.*

Peppered Pork Loin

Deanna Robinson, Robson, WV

This roast pork makes delicious sandwiches! Slice leftovers to desired thickness and fry in a skillet coated with non-stick vegetable spray.

1/2 t. pepper
1/2 t. garlic and pepper seasoning salt
1/2 t. Cajun seasoning
4 to 6-lb. boneless pork loin

Mix together seasonings and rub into pork loin. Wrap in 2 sheets of heavy-duty aluminum foil, sealing well. Place on a baking sheet. Bake at 350 degrees for 1-1/2 to 2 hours. Let stand 15 minutes before slicing. Makes 14 servings.

Make-ahead directions: *Prepare roast for baking and refrigerate until ready to bake the next day.*

Lisa's Chicken Tortilla Soup

Lisa's Chicken Tortilla Soup

This easy-to-make soup will warm their tummies on a cold, cold night.

4 14-1/2 oz. cans chicken broth
4 10-oz. cans diced tomatoes with green chiles
1 c. canned or frozen corn
30-oz. can refried beans
5 c. cooked chicken, shredded
Garnish: shredded Mexican-blend or Monterey Jack
  cheese, corn chips or tortilla strips

In a large stockpot over medium heat, combine broth and tomatoes with chiles. Stir in corn and beans; bring to a boil. Reduce heat to low and simmer for 5 to 10 minutes, stirring frequently. Add chicken and heat through. To serve, garnish as desired. Serves 10.

Make-ahead directions: *Prepare as directed. Cool; do not garnish. Ladle into a freezer-safe container and freeze. To serve, thaw overnight in refrigerator. In a saucepan, simmer over medium heat until hot and bubbly. Garnish as desired.*

Quick tip

Just for fun, serve a variety of corn chips with soups or salads. Make it a taste test and keep track of the favorites.

Maple Pork Chops

Emma Brown, Saskatchewan, Canada

The sweetness of the maple syrup and saltiness of the soy sauce go so well together. My family can't get enough of these...I usually have to double the recipe!

1/2 c. maple syrup
3 T. soy sauce
2 cloves garlic, minced
4 pork chops

In a bowl, whisk together syrup, soy sauce and garlic; reserve 1/4 cup of mixture. Add pork chops to remaining mixture in bowl. Cover and refrigerate for at least 15 minutes to overnight. Drain, discarding mixture in bowl. Grill over medium-high heat until browned and cooked through, about 6 minutes per side. Drizzle pork chops with reserved syrup mixture before serving. Makes 4 servings.

Make-ahead directions: *Prepare recipe as instructed and refrigerate overnight until ready to grill the next day.*

Maple Pork Chops

Fruity Baked Chicken

Fruity Baked Chicken

Jennifer Holmes, Philadelphia, PA

Serve over rice with a side of asparagus spears...yum.

2 T. olive oil
6 boneless, skinless chicken breasts
3 lemons, halved
3 oranges, halved
1 apple, peeled, cored and chopped

Coat the bottom of a 13"x9" baking pan with olive oil; arrange chicken breasts on top. Squeeze juice from one lemon and one orange over chicken; set aside. Slice remaining lemons and oranges into wedges; cut these in half. Arrange around and on top of chicken breasts; add apple. Cover and bake at 350 degrees for one hour and 45 minutes; uncover for last 30 minutes of baking. Makes 6 servings.

Make-ahead directions: *Prepare recipe as directed but do not bake. Cover and refrigerate until ready to bake the next day following baking instructions.*

Granny's Macaroni Salad

Granny's Macaroni Salad

Suzanne Morrow, Moorhead, MN

My family loves this cheesy macaroni salad made from my grandmother's own recipe. She was a very good granny to me!

48-oz. pkg. macaroni shells, uncooked
8-oz. pkg. pasteurized process cheese, cubed
1 green pepper, chopped
1 cucumber, shredded
4 to 5 carrots, peeled and shredded
2 tomatoes, chopped

Cook macaroni according to package directions. Drain and rinse with cold water. In a large serving bowl, mix cheese and vegetables together; add macaroni. Toss together. Add Salad Dressing and mix well. Refrigerate 8 hours to overnight to allow flavors to combine. Serves 15 to 20.

Salad Dressing:
2 c. mayonnaise-style salad dressing
2 T. sugar
2 T. vinegar
1 T. mustard
Mix together in a small bowl.

Make-ahead directions: *Prepare as directed. Refrigerate until ready to serve the next day.*

Make-Ahead Tomato Soup

Make-Ahead Tomato Soup

Gretchen Ham, Pine City, NY

Fresh basil really makes this soup special. The flavors get even better when it is warmed up the next day!

1/2 c. butter, sliced
1 c. fresh basil, chopped
2 28-oz. cans crushed tomatoes
2 cloves garlic, minced
1 qt. half-and-half
salt and pepper to taste
Garnish: fresh parsley, sliced cherry tomatoes, croutons

In a large saucepan, melt butter over medium heat. Add basil; sauté for 2 minutes. Add tomatoes and garlic; reduce heat and simmer for 20 minutes. Remove from heat; let cool slightly. Working in batches, transfer tomato mixture to a blender and purée. Strain into a separate saucepan and add half-and-half, mixing very well. Reheat soup over medium-low heat; add salt and pepper to taste. Garnish as desired. Makes 10 servings.

Make-ahead directions: *Prepare soup as instructed. Cool and refrigerate until ready to use. Heat through when ready to use. Soup will keep refrigerated for up to 3 days.*

Parmesan Baked Pork Chops

Coleen Lambert. Luxemburg, WI

These luscious pork chops just melt in your mouth.

1 c. Italian-flavored dry bread crumbs
1 c. grated Parmesan cheese
1 t. garlic powder
1 t. pepper
1 T. olive oil
4 boneless pork chops, 1/2-inch thick

Mix bread crumbs, Parmesan cheese and seasonings in a shallow dish. Brush olive oil over pork chops and press into crumb mixture, coating well on both sides. Arrange pork chops in a greased 13"x9" baking pan. Bake, uncovered, at 350 degrees for 40 to 45 minutes, until pork chops are tender and golden. Makes 4 servings.

Make-ahead directions: *Prepare recipe as directed but do not bake. Cover and refrigerate. Uncover and bake as directed the next day.*

Parmesan Baked Pork Chops

Overnight Scalloped Turkey

This make-ahead recipe is perfect to prepare on Sunday to have ready for baking for that busy Monday evening meal.

2 10-3/4 oz. cans cream of mushroom soup
2-1/2 c. milk
8-oz. pkg. pasteurized process cheese spread, cubed
4 c. cooked turkey, chopped
7-oz pkg. elbow macaroni, uncooked
1-1/2 c. soft bread crumbs

Combine soup, milk and cheese in a large bowl; add turkey and macaroni. Transfer to a lightly greased 13"x9" baking pan. Cover and refrigerate for 8 hours or overnight. Sprinkle bread crumbs on top. Bake, uncovered, at 350 degrees for 45 to 50 minutes. Serves 8 to 10.

Make-ahead directions: *Prepare recipe; cover and refrigerate until ready to bake the next day. Bake as directed.*

Light & Fluffy Pancakes

Everyone loves pancakes, but when time is short, pancakes can keep the cook in the kitchen too long! These fluffy pancakes can be made ahead and frozen. They warm up beautifully and everyone is happy!

1 c. all-purpose flour
2 T. sugar
2 t. baking powder
1/2 t. salt
1 egg, beaten
1 c. milk
2 T. oil
Garnish: fresh raspberries, whipped cream or powdered sugar

Stir together flour, sugar, baking powder and salt. Add egg, milk and oil all at once to flour mixture, stirring until blended but still slightly lumpy. Pour batter onto a hot, lightly greased griddle or heavy skillet, about 1/4 cup each for regular pancakes or one tablespoon for silver dollar pancakes. Cook on both sides until golden, turning when surface is bubbly and edges are slightly dry. Garnish as desired. Makes 6 to 8 servings

Make-ahead directions: *Cool; do not garnish. Store in freezer bags. To serve, place frozen pancakes in a single layer on a baking sheet. Cover with aluminum foil; bake at 350 degrees for about 10 minutes.*

Quick tip

Make your own healthier homemade bread crumbs using whole-grain bread. Let the bread dry out slightly and then use a food processor to make the crumbs.

Light & Fluffy Pancakes

Simple Baked Mostaccioli

Simple Baked Mostaccioli

Michele Molen, Mendon, UT

16-oz. pkg. mostaccioli pasta, uncooked
1 lb. ground beef
salt and pepper to taste
16-oz. jar pasta sauce, divided
8-oz. pkg. shredded mozzarella cheese, divided

Cook pasta according to package directions; drain. Meanwhile, brown beef in a skillet over medium heat. Drain; season with salt and pepper. Ladle a spoonful of pasta sauce into a greased 2-quart casserole dish; add half of cooked pasta. Layer with all of beef mixture, half of remaining sauce and half of cheese; repeat layers with remaining pasta, sauce and cheese. Bake, uncovered, at 375 degrees for about 20 minutes, until hot and bubbly. Serves 5.

Make-ahead directions: *Prepare recipe, but do not bake. Cover and refrigerate until ready to bake the next day. Bake as directed.*

My Italian grandmother always used this quick & easy recipe when she needed a dish for last-minute company or to send to a sick friend. It will always be a comfort food to me...mangia, mangia! —Michele

Sassy Spaghetti Sauce

Dina Willard, Abingdon, MD

The best thing about this sassy sauce is how easy it is to prepare! Sometimes pasta sauces can be boring, so I came up with this quick version that's great for busy weeknights. Top with freshly grated Parmesan cheese for a meal that can't be beat.

32-oz. pkg. spaghetti, uncooked
2 14-1/2 oz. cans Italian-style diced tomatoes
7-oz. jar roasted red peppers, drained
7-oz. jar Kalamata olives, drained
6-oz. jar marinated artichokes, drained
1/2 c. grated Parmesan cheese

Cook spaghetti according to package directions; drain and return to cooking pot. Meanwhile, in a large saucepan over medium heat, stir together remaining ingredients. Bring to a boil. Reduce heat to low; simmer for 15 minutes, stirring occasionally. Add sauce to spaghetti and mix gently. Makes 6 servings.

Make-ahead directions: *Cook sauce as directed. Place in freezer-safe container and freeze until ready to use. Sauce will keep in freezer for up to 2 months. Or, if using the next day, refrigerate and heat when serving. Cook pasta when ready to serve sauce.*

Lizzy's Make-Ahead Egg Casserole

Lizzy Burnley, Ankeny, IA

This recipe is a favorite for breakfast, lunch or dinner! And preparing it ahead makes it that much easier!

1 doz. eggs, beaten
1 c. cooked ham, diced
3 c. whole milk
12 frozen waffles
2 c. shredded Cheddar cheese

In a large bowl, beat eggs. Stir in ham and milk. Grease a 13"x9" baking pan. Place one layer of waffles in the bottom of the pan. Pour half of the mixture on the waffles. Sprinkle with half of the cheese. Continue layering waffles, egg mixture and cheese. Cover and refrigerate overnight. Uncover and bake at 350 degrees for about one hour or until eggs are set. Serves 12.

Make-ahead directions: *Prepare recipe; cover and refrigerate until ready to bake the next day. Bake as directed.*

Lizzy's Make-Ahead Egg Casserole

Pepperoni & Cheese Quiche

This pizza-like, no-shell quiche will be a favorite for the entire family. Make 2 and freeze one for later.

2 eggs, beaten
3/4 c. all-purpose flour
1 c. milk
1/2 t. salt
1/8 t. pepper
1/2 c. Muenster cheese, shredded
1/2 c. shredded Cheddar cheese
1/4 c. pepperoni, finely chopped

Whisk together first 5 ingredients. Stir in cheeses and pepperoni. Pour into an ungreased 8" pie plate; bake at 375 degrees for 30 minutes, or until puffy and golden.

Make-ahead directions: *Bake as directed; cool, wrap and freeze whole or sliced. To serve, thaw in refrigerator for several hours to overnight. Bake at 350 degrees for a few minutes, until warmed through.*

Quick tip

A quiche recipe can be altered to include your family's favorite flavors. Use the same amount of eggs, milk and flour and then choose your favorite cheese, herbs and chopped meat.

Pepperoni & Cheese Quiche

Busy-Night Burgers & Sandwiches

(with must-have sides)

These yummy burgers and sandwiches are perfect for busy weeknights or special game or movie nights. Jazz up your supper with Marty's Special Burgers filled with blue cheese and cherry tomatoes. Add a side of Homestyle Butterbeans for a complete meal. Want a cold sandwich? A little honey-nut cream cheese makes Sweet Smoky Sandwiches extra special. Fire up the stove and present your family with Grilled Havarti Sandwiches with a side of Minted Baby Carrots. Your family will love these mouthwatering sandwich-style meals that you make with 6 ingredients or less!

Tex-Mex Burgers

The chips in these burgers make them unusually good!

2 lbs. ground beef
1 c. shredded Cheddar cheese
1/2 c. onion, grated
1/2 c. salsa
2 to 3 c. tortilla chips, crushed
8 sandwich buns, split

In a bowl, combine all ingredients except buns; shape into patties. Grill over medium heat to desired doneness. Serve on buns. Makes 8 burgers.

Avocado Egg Salad Sandwiches

Crystal Bruns, Iliff, CO

A fresh and delicious twist on egg salad...serve it on your favorite hearty bread!

6 eggs, hard-boiled, peeled and chopped
2 avocados, halved, pitted and cubed
1/4 c. red onion, minced
1/3 c. mayonnaise
1 T. mustard
salt and pepper to taste
12 slices bread

Mash eggs with a fork in a bowl until crumbly. Add remaining ingredients except bread slices. Gently mix together until blended. Spread egg mixture evenly over 6 bread slices. Top with remaining bread slices. Makes 6 sandwiches.

California Pita Sandwiches

Gladys Kielar, Whitehouse, OH

1 pita round, halved and split
1 avocado, halved, pitted and sliced
1 tomato, sliced
1 slice Swiss cheese, halved
several leaves Romaine lettuce
Thousand Island salad dressing to taste

Fill each half of pita with avocado, tomato, cheese, lettuce leaves and dressing to taste. Makes 2 sandwiches.

I first tasted this yummy sandwich while on vacation in California. Now I make my own. Ripe avocado and fresh tomato slices make all the difference. So delicious and easy! Serve with fresh fruit for a compete meal! —Gladys

California Pita Sandwiches

Grilled Havarti Sandwiches

Bev Fisher, Mesa, AZ

Now that my children are grown, I'm always looking for recipes that call for ingredients they wouldn't eat. This sandwich is so tasty, I wanted another one the next day after I first tried it!

8 slices French bread
2 t. butter, softened and divided
4 T. apricot preserves
1/4 lb. Havarti cheese, sliced
1 avocado, halved, pitted and sliced

Spread 4 slices bread on one side with half the butter and all the preserves. Top with cheese, avocado and another slice of bread; spread remaining butter on outside of sandwiches. Heat a large skillet over medium heat. Cook sandwiches for 2 to 3 minutes, until bread is golden and cheese begins to melt. Turn over; press down slightly with a spatula. Cook until golden. Makes 4 sandwiches.

Grilled Havarti Sandwiches

Minted Baby Carrots

Mini Ham & Cheesewiches

Elisa Thompson, Celina, TN

I always take these little sandwiches to family gatherings. I have a very large family, so I have to fix lots!

17-oz. pkg. brown & serve dinner rolls
8-oz. pkg. sliced deli ham
12 slices American cheese
Garnish: melted butter, garlic salt

Slice each roll in half like a hamburger bun. Place a slice of ham and a slice of cheese on each roll bottom. Add tops; brush with butter and sprinkle with garlic salt. Arrange on an ungreased baking sheet. Bake at 450 degrees until golden and cheese is melted. Makes one dozen.

Minted Baby Carrots

Tori Willis, Champaign, IL

1/2 lb. baby carrots
1 T. butter
salt and pepper to taste
1 T. lemon zest, minced
1 T. brown sugar, packed
2 t. fresh mint, minced

In a stockpot of boiling water, cook carrots 5 minutes. Remove from heat, and drain. Melt butter in a skillet over medium-high heat. Stir in carrots; cook until crisp-tender. Season with salt and pepper to taste. Combine remaining ingredients, and sprinkle over individual servings. Serves 4.

Mint is so easy to grow. Plant some in your garden and you'll have it come back every year! Or keep some growing in a sunny spot by the kitchen door, and you can whip up these yummy carrots anytime. —Tori

So-Good Turkey Burgers

So-Good Turkey Burgers

Ground turkey is spiced up a bit with Italian seasonings and Worcestershire sauce. Yum!

1 lb. ground turkey
2 T. fresh chives, chopped
1/2 c. Italian-flavored dry bread crumbs
1/4 c. Worcestershire sauce
1/2 t. dry mustard
salt and pepper to taste
4 to 6 hamburger buns, split

Combine all ingredients except buns; form into 4 to 6 patties. Grill to desired doneness; serve on hamburger buns. Makes 4 to 6 sandwiches.

Homemade Bagels

Kathy's Denver Sandwich

Kathrine Moore, British Columbia, Canada

This is my idea of a good and easy sandwich! Now that I look after my mother who can't see any more, it's very important to find recipes that can be made into a sandwich for her. You can substitute ham for bacon or change around the veggies to your liking.

4 slices bacon, chopped
1 T. onion, chopped
2 T. green pepper, chopped
3 eggs, beaten
1/4 c. shredded Cheddar cheese
6 slices bread, toasted and buttered

In a skillet over medium heat, cook bacon until partially done but not crisp. Add onion and green pepper; cook until softened. Add eggs and cook to desired doneness. Sprinkle with cheese; cover and let stand until melted. Cut into 3 pieces; serve each between 2 slices of toast. Makes 3 sandwiches.

Homemade Bagels

These are great for sandwiches of any kind! Try cream cheese with thinly-sliced ham for a yummy and quick treat.

1 env. active dry yeast
1 c. warm water
2 T. sugar
1-1/2 t. salt
2-3/4 c. all-purpose flour, divided
Garnish: cream cheese

In a large bowl, dissolve yeast in very warm water, 110 to 115 degrees. Add sugar, salt and half the flour to the yeast mixture; mix until smooth. Stir in remaining flour. Knead dough for 10 minutes on a lightly floured surface. Cover and let rise in a warm place until double in bulk. Punch down and divide into 8 equal pieces. Form each piece into a doughnut shape; let rise for 20 minutes. Bring a large pot of water to a boil; add bagels and boil for 7 minutes, turning once. Remove from water and place on a greased baking sheet. Bake at 375 degrees for 30 to 35 minutes, until golden. Cool slightly; slice and top with cream cheese. Makes 8 bagels.

Louisiana Sausage Sandwiches

Louisiana Sausage Sandwiches

The peppers and onions add just the right flavor to the spicy sausages in this tasty sandwich.

19.76-oz. pkg. Italian pork sausage links
1 green pepper, sliced into bite-size pieces
1 onion, sliced into bite-size pieces
8-oz. can tomato sauce
1/8 t. pepper
6 hoagie rolls, split

In a large skillet, brown sausage links over medium heat. Cut into 1/2-inch slices. Stir in remaining ingredients except rolls. Cover and simmer for about 30 minutes until sausages are cooked. Spoon into rolls with a slotted spoon. Makes 6 sandwiches.

Tangy Turkey Salad Croissants

Wendy Jacobs, Idaho Falls, ID

2 c. cooked turkey breast, cubed
1 orange, peeled and chopped
1/2 c. cranberries, finely chopped
1/2 c. mayonnaise
1/2 t. salt
1/4 c. chopped pecans
6 croissants, split
Garnish: lettuce leaves

Combine turkey, orange, cranberries, mayonnaise and salt; chill. Stir in pecans before serving. Top each croissant half with 1/2 cup turkey mixture and a lettuce leaf. Top with remaining croissant half. Makes 6 sandwiches.

The day after Thanksgiving, my mom, sisters and I decided we wanted more than just the usual turkey sandwich. We combined some of our favorite flavors and came up with these turkey croissant sandwiches. We love them! —Wendy

Tangy Turkey Salad Croissants

Marty's Special Burgers

The blue cheese in these burgers is the secret!

1 lb. lean ground beef
1/2 c. crumbled feta or blue cheese
1/2 c. bread crumbs
1 egg, beaten
1/2 t. salt
1/4 t. pepper
4 to 6 cherry tomatoes, halved
4 hamburger buns, split

Mix together all ingredients except buns; form into 4 burgers. Grill over high heat to desired doneness, flipping to cook on both sides. Serve on buns. Makes 4 sandwiches.

Creamy Tuna Sandwiches

Phyllis Peters, Three Rivers, MI

A quick, simple dinner to prepare when time is short.

6-oz. can tuna, drained
10-3/4 oz. can cream of mushroom soup
1/4 c. milk
1 c. frozen peas, cooked
6 English muffins, halved and toasted

Combine ingredients except muffins in a saucepan; bring to a boil. Spoon over bottom halves of English muffins; add top half. Serve warm. Makes 6 servings.

Marty's Special Burgers

Homestyle Butterbeans

Homestyle Butterbeans

Use this recipe for lima beans, too! Serve with your favorite burger for a hearty meal.

5 bacon slices, diced
1 onion, minced
1/2 c. brown sugar, packed
16-oz. pkg. frozen butterbeans
1/4 c. butter
1 c. water
1 t. salt
1 t. pepper

Cook bacon and onion in a large Dutch oven over medium heat for 5 to 7 minutes. Add brown sugar; cook stirring occasionally, one to 2 minutes or until sugar is dissolved. Stir in butterbeans and butter until butter is melted and beans are thoroughly coated. Stir in water. Bring to a boil over medium-high heat; reduce heat to low. Simmer, stirring occasionally, 10 to 15 minutes or until beans are very tender and liquid is thickened. Stir in salt and pepper. Serves 6 to 8.

Raspberry-Dijon Baguettes

Deborah Lomax, Peoria, IL

Pair grilled chicken breasts with a tangy-sweet sauce on French bread...a masterpiece!

1 baguette, sliced into 8 slices
Dijon mustard to taste
raspberry jam to taste
4 boneless, skinless chicken breasts, grilled and sliced
2 c. arugula leaves
Optional: red onion slices

Spread 4 slices of baguette with mustard. Top remaining slices with raspberry jam. Arrange a layer of grilled chicken over mustard; top with arugula and onion, if desired. Cover with remaining baguette slices. Serves 4.

Quick tip

Toast buns slightly before adding the burger or sliced meats...it takes only a minute and makes such a tasty difference.

BBQ Chicken Calzones

Refrigerated pizza dough makes these calzones so easy to make!

12-oz. tube refrigerated pizza dough
3 c. cooked chicken, diced
1 c. barbecue sauce
1 c. shredded mozzarella cheese
1 egg, beaten
1 t. water

On a floured surface, roll dough to 1/2-inch thickness; cut into 2 rectangles and place on ungreased baking sheets. In a bowl, combine chicken and barbecue sauce. For each calzone, spoon half the chicken mixture onto one half of the dough. Top with half the cheese. Fold over dough and seal the edges. Mix together egg and water. Use a pastry brush to brush egg mixture over each calzone; use a knife to cut 3 slits in the tops. Bake at 400 degrees for 25 minutes, or until golden. Makes 4 servings.

BBQ Chicken Calzones

Triple-Take Grilled Cheese

This impressive sandwich is sure to be a hit with the kids!

1 T. oil
8 slices sourdough bread
1/4 c. butter, softened and divided
4 slices American cheese
4 slices Muenster cheese
1/2 c. shredded sharp Cheddar cheese
Optional: 4 slices red onion, 4 slices tomato,
   1/4 c. chopped fresh basil

Heat oil in a skillet over medium heat. Spread 2 bread slices with one tablespoon butter; place one slice butter-side down on skillet. Layer one slice American, one slice Muenster and 2 tablespoons Cheddar cheese on bread. If desired, top with an onion slice, a tomato slice and one tablespoon basil. Place second buttered bread slice on top of sandwich in skillet. Reduce heat to medium-low. Cook until golden on one side, about 3 to 5 minutes; flip and cook until golden on the other side. Repeat with remaining ingredients. Makes 4 sandwiches.

Quick tip

When making grilled cheese sandwiches, try different kinds of cheeses such as Havarti or Swiss. They melt well and taste great!

Triple-Take Grilled Cheese

Dad's Wimpy Burgers

In a large bowl, combine beef, catsup, egg, onion and salt; mix well. Form into 6 to 8 patties. Place bread crumbs in a shallow pan. Pat each side of patties in crumbs until coated. Place patties in a lightly greased 13"x9" baking pan. Bake, uncovered, at 350 degrees for 20 to 25 minutes, flipping patties after 8 minutes. Patties may also be pan-fried in a lightly greased skillet over medium heat. Cook on each side for 6 to 8 minutes, until lightly browned. Serve on buns. Makes 6 to 8 servings.

Easy Sloppy Joes

Instant brown rice makes this Sloppy Joe easy to make and a little bit healthier.

1-1/2 lbs. ground beef
1 T. beef bouillon granules
1/2 c. instant brown rice, uncooked
1/4 c. catsup
1/2 c. water
salt and pepper to taste
6 hamburger buns, split

Brown beef in a skillet until all pink in beef is gone. Drain and return to skillet. Add remaining ingredients except buns and bring to a boil. Boil for one minute. Remove from heat and cover for 10 minutes. Serve on hamburger buns. Serves 6.

Dad's Wimpy Burgers

These hearty sandwiches will fill up the biggest kid at the table. Serve with a green veggie for a complete meal.

2 lbs. ground beef
1/2 c. catsup
1 egg, beaten
1 onion, chopped
1/2 t. salt
1 c. Italian-flavored dry bread crumbs
6 to 8 hamburger buns, split

Easy Sloppy Joes

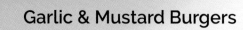
Garlic & Mustard Burgers

Garlic & Mustard Burgers

No one will be able to resist these tasty burgers!

1 lb. ground beef
3 T. country-style Dijon mustard
4 cloves garlic, chopped
4 Monterey Jack cheese slices
7-oz. jar roasted red peppers, drained
4 hamburger buns, split and toasted

Mix together beef, mustard and garlic. Shape mixture into 4 patties about 3/4-inch thick. Cover and grill patties for 12 to 15 minutes, to desired doneness. Top with cheese and peppers. Serve on toasted buns. Serves 4.

Excellent Burgers

Carrie Kelderman, Pella, IA

1 lb. lean ground beef
1 lb. ground pork
2 eggs, beaten
1-1/2 oz. pkg. spaghetti sauce mix
8 hamburger buns, split

Combine all ingredients together except buns. Mix well, and form into 8 patties. Grill over hot coals to desired doneness. Place on buns. Serves 8.

Green Bean Sauté

Emily Martin, Ontario, Canada

A simple side dish that comes together in a jiffy.

1/2 onion, cut into thin wedges
1 clove garlic, minced
1/2 t. dried basil
1 T. olive oil
2 14-1/2 oz. cans green beans, drained
14-1/2 oz. can petite diced tomatoes, drained

In a saucepan over medium heat, combine onion, garlic, basil and oil. Sauté for about 5 minutes, until onion is tender. Add green beans and tomatoes; heat through. Makes 4 to 6 servings.

Weeknight Treat Burgers

Marie Warner, Jennings, FL

My husband loves big half-pound burgers, but you could make eight smaller burgers if your family's appetites are lighter. Top these burgers with sautéed mushrooms for an extra-special meal.

2/3 c. shredded provolone cheese
1/2 c. green pepper, diced
1/2 c. onion, chopped
salt and pepper to taste
2 lbs. ground beef chuck
4 sesame seed Kaiser rolls

Toss together cheese, green pepper, onion, salt and pepper in a large bowl. Add ground beef; mix well, and form into 4 patties. Fry in a skillet over medium-high heat for 4 to 5 minutes on each side, or until desired doneness. Serve on rolls. Serves 4.

Grilled Panini

Baby PB&J Bagel Sandwiches

These bagels put a crunchy spin on a childhood favorite!

6 mini bagels, split
6 T. creamy peanut butter
6 t. strawberry or grape jelly
1 T. butter, melted

Spread peanut butter evenly on cut sides of bottom halves of bagels; spread jelly evenly on cut sides of top halves of bagels. Place top halves of bagels on bottom halves, jelly sides down. Brush bagels lightly with melted butter; cook in a preheated panini press 2 minutes or until lightly golden and grill marks appear. Serve immediately. Serves 6.

Grilled Panini

Tina Goodpasture, Meadowview, VA

2 slices sourdough bread
1 T. mayonnaise
6 slices deli smoked ham
2 slices tomato
1 slice Cheddar cheese

Spread both slices of bread with mayonnaise on one side. Top one slice with ham, tomato, cheese and remaining bread slice. Spray a griddle or skillet with non-stick vegetable spray. Place ham sandwich on griddle or in preheated panini press. Cook sandwich, turning once over medium heat for about 5 minutes or until lightly golden on both sides. Makes one sandwich.

Treat yourself to this fast-fix sandwich on a busy night. A griddle or panini press works great for this yummy sandwich! —Tina

Spicy Sweet Potato Fries

Spicy Sweet Potato Fries

Change up the sides you serve by making these sweet potato fries with just a touch of spice. They'll love them!

2 lbs. sweet potatoes, peeled and cut into wedges or strips
3 T. olive oil, divided
1 t. seasoned salt
1 t. ground cumin
1/2 t. chili powder
1/2 t. pepper
Optional: ranch salad dressing

Place sweet potatoes in a plastic zipping bag. Sprinkle with 2 tablespoons oil and seasonings; toss to coat. Drizzle remaining oil over a baking sheet; place sweet potatoes in a single layer on sheet. Bake, uncovered, at 425 degrees for 25 to 35 minutes, turning halfway through cooking time, until sweet potatoes are golden. Serve with salad dressing for dipping if desired. Makes 4 to 6 servings.

Texas Steak Sandwiches

Texas Steak Sandwiches

The family will love this thick-toasted sandwich!

8 slices frozen Texas toast
1-1/2 lbs. deli roast beef, sliced
steak sauce to taste
8 slices provolone cheese
Optional: sliced green pepper and red onion, sautéed

Bake Texas toast on a baking sheet at 425 degrees for about 5 minutes per side, until softened and lightly golden; set aside. Warm roast beef in a skillet over medium heat until most of the juices have evaporated; stir in steak sauce. Divide beef evenly among 4 toast slices; top with cheese, pepper and onion, if desired. Place beef-topped toast and remaining toast on a baking sheet; bake at 425 degrees until cheese is melted. Combine to form sandwiches. Makes 4 sandwiches.

Quick tip

If you have problems peeling hard-boiled eggs, try running them under cold water while you are peeling them. It works like a charm!

Egg Salad Sandwiches

Julie Ann Perkins, Anderson, IN

This recipe is sure to please...it is quick, easy and delicious! Family & friends welcome this comfort food, and it gives you more time to spend in the garden, on the porch or at the fruit market!

7 eggs, hard-boiled, peeled and diced
3 green onions, diced
1 stalk celery, diced
1 T. horseradish mustard
1/3 to 1/2 c. olive oil mayonnaise
salt and pepper to taste
bread, toast, bagels or crackers

In a large bowl, combine eggs, onions, celery and mustard. Stir in mayonnaise to desired consistency. Add salt and pepper to taste. Mix until smooth and well blended. Serve on bread, toast, bagels or crackers. Makes 4 servings.

Wanda's Wimpies

Wanda Leuty, Swansen, IL

An easy Sloppy Joe recipe for busy parents and grandparents.

1-1/2 lbs. lean ground beef
salt and pepper to taste
10-3/4 oz. can tomato soup
1/2 c. tangy-flavored catsup
6 to 8 sandwich buns

Brown beef in a heavy saucepan; salt and pepper to taste. Add soup and catsup; reduce heat and simmer until thick. Spoon onto buns to serve. Makes 6 to 8 servings.

Favorite Egg Muffins

This rich egg recipe is perfect on a cold winter night.

10-3/4 oz. can Cheddar cheese soup
1-1/2 c. milk
4 eggs
4 slices Canadian bacon
4 English muffins, split and toasted
3 T. butter, divided

In a bowl, mix together soup and milk. Fill 4 greased custard cups 1/4 full with soup mixture. Set cups on a baking sheet. Crack an egg into each cup, being careful not to break the yolks. Bake cups at 350 degrees for 12 minutes. Meanwhile, brown both sides of bacon in a skillet over medium heat. Top each muffin half with one teaspoon butter. Place 4 muffin halves on a baking sheet. Top each with a slice of bacon. Turn out a baked egg onto each bacon-topped muffin half. Drizzle remaining cheese sauce over each egg. Top with other halves of muffins. Bake for an additional 2 minutes, or until heated through. Makes 4 servings.

Rise & Shine Sandwiches

Dale Duncan, Waterloo, IA

My family loves breakfast sandwiches for dinner. They're easy to make and easy to adapt to your own tastes!

2-1/4 c. buttermilk biscuit baking mix
1/2 c. water
8 pork sausage breakfast patties
8 eggs, beaten
1 T. butter
salt and pepper to taste
8 slices American cheese

In a bowl, combine biscuit mix with water until just blended. Turn onto a floured surface and knead for one minute. Roll dough out to 1/2-inch thickness. Cut out 8 biscuits with a 3-inch round biscuit cutter. Arrange on an ungreased baking sheet. Bake at 425 degrees for 8 to 10 minutes, until golden. Meanwhile, in a skillet over medium heat, brown and cook sausage patties; drain. In a separate skillet over low heat, scramble eggs in butter to desired doneness; season with salt and pepper. Split biscuits; top each biscuit bottom with a sausage patty, a spoonful of eggs and a cheese slice. Add biscuit tops and serve immediately. Makes 8 servings.

Quick tip

Serve a breakfast-style meal for dinner at least once a week. Bring out the orange juice and fruit. Then have ice cream for dessert!

Rise & Shine Sandwiches

Caesar Focaccia Sandwich

Wendy Ball, Battle Creek, MI

2 c. mixed salad greens
1/4 c. Caesar salad dressing
8-inch round focaccia bread, halved horizontally
4 slices Cheddar cheese
1/2 lb. deli turkey, thinly shaved
1 tomato, sliced

Toss salad greens with salad dressing; set aside. Layer bottom half of focaccia with greens mixture and remaining ingredients. Add top half of focaccia; cut into halves or quarters. Serves 2 to 4.

Pepper Steak Sammies

Vickie

1 to 1-1/4 lbs. beef sirloin or ribeye steak
2 green peppers, thinly sliced
1 onion, sliced
1 T. oil
salt and pepper to taste
1/4 c. garlic butter, softened
4 French rolls, split and toasted

Grill or broil steak to desired doneness; set aside. Sauté green peppers and onion in hot oil in a skillet over medium heat until crisp-tender; drain. Slice steak thinly; add to skillet and heat through. Sprinkle with salt and pepper. Spread butter over cut sides of rolls. Spoon steak mixture onto bottom halves of rolls; cover with tops. Makes 4 sandwiches.

Scott's Ham & Pear Sandwiches

The sweetness of the pear combined with the salty ham makes for a much-requested sandwich!

8 slices sourdough bread
4 slices Swiss cheese
1-1/4 lbs. sliced deli ham
15-oz. can pear halves, drained and thinly sliced

Spread each bread slice with a thin layer of Spiced Butter. On each of 4 slices, place one slice of cheese; layer evenly with ham and pears. Top with remaining bread slices and press together gently. Spread the outside of the sandwiches with Spiced Butter. Heat a large skillet over medium-high heat and cook until crisp and golden, about 5 minutes on each side. Makes 4 sandwiches.

Spiced Butter:
1 c. butter, softened
2 t. pumpkin pie spice
1 t. ground coriander
1 t. ground ginger
1 t. salt

Combine all ingredients until smooth and evenly mixed. Use as a sandwich spread.

Scott's Ham & Pear Sandwiches

Sweet Smoky Sandwiches

Sweet Smoky Sandwiches

Add pizzazz to the common turkey sandwich with a sour apple and honey-nut cream cheese spread.

2 Granny Smith apples, cored and cut into thin slices
2 T. lemon juice
1/2 c. honey-nut cream cheese
8 whole-grain bread slices
1/2 c. dried cranberries
3/4 lb. deli smoked turkey breast, sliced thin

Toss apple slices with lemon juice; drain. Spread cream cheese evenly on one side of each bread slice; top 4 slices of bread evenly with apple slices, cranberries and turkey. Cover with remaining bread slices, cream cheese-side down. Makes 4.

Herb Garden Sandwiches

Lynda Robson, Boston, MA

These might seem like delicate sandwiches, but serve with a hearty tomato soup and you have a quick meal.

8-oz. pkg. cream cheese, softened
1/2 c. fresh herbs, finely chopped, such as parsley,
  watercress, basil, chervil, chives
1 t. lemon juice
1/8 t. hot pepper sauce
8 slices whole-wheat bread, crusts removed
paprika to taste

Combine all ingredients except bread and paprika. Spread cream cheese mixture evenly over half of bread slices. Sprinkle with paprika. Top with remaining bread slices; slice diagonally into quarters. Makes 16 sandwiches.

Monster Meatball Sandwiches

Make plenty of these sandwiches...they'll love them!

32 frozen bite-size meatballs
9-oz. jar mango chutney
1 c. chicken broth
16 dinner rolls
16-oz jar sweet-hot pickle sandwich relish

Stir together first 3 ingredients in a medium saucepan. Bring to a boil over medium-high heat. Reduce heat to low and simmer, stirring occasionally, 25 to 30 minutes. Cut rolls vertically through top, cutting to, but not through bottom. Place 2 meatballs in each roll. Top with relish. Makes 16.

Monster Meatball Sandwiches

Toasted Green Tomato Sandwiches

Janie Reed, Zanesville, OH

Heat up your skillet to make this hot, buttery favorite.
Tomatoes never tasted better...yum!

1-1/2 to 2 c. cornmeal
salt, pepper and seasoning salt to taste
2 green tomatoes, sliced 1/4-inch thick
oil or shortening for frying
2 to 3 T. butter, softened
8 slices whole-wheat bread
Optional: basil mayonnaise, curly leaf lettuce

Combine cornmeal and seasonings in a large plastic
zipping bag. Shake to mix well. Add tomato slices, and
gently shake to coat. Remove tomatoes from bag, shaking
off excess cornmeal mixture. Heat oil or shortening in a
large skillet over medium heat; fry tomatoes until golden
on both sides. Remove from skillet. Spread butter on
one side of each bread slice. Arrange 4 slices, butter-side
down, in skillet. Cook over medium heat until toasted.
Repeat with remaining bread slices. Spread mayonnaise
over untoasted sides of bread, if desired. Top with
tomatoes and lettuce, if desired. Close sandwich with
another slice of bread. Cook sandwiches over medium
heat, turning once, until golden on both sides. Serves 4.

Extra-Cheesy Grilled Cheese

Delicious in winter with a steaming bowl of tomato soup
and scrumptious in summer made with produce fresh from
the garden!

4 t. butter, softened
4 slices French bread
2 slices provolone cheese
2 slices mozzarella cheese
2 slices red onion
2 slices tomato
Optional: fresh basil leaves

Spread one teaspoon butter on each of 4 bread slices.
Place 2 bread slices, butter-side down, in a large skillet or
on a hot griddle. Layer one slice provolone and one slice
mozzarella cheese on each bread slice. Top with an
onion slice, tomato slice and basil leaf if using. Top with
a bread slice butter-side up. Reduce heat to medium low.
Cook until golden on one side, about 3 to 5 minutes; flip
and cook until golden on other side. Makes 2 sandwiches.

Toasted Green Tomato Sandwiches

Extra-Cheesy Grilled Cheese

Peanut Butter Apple-Bacon Sandwich

Irene Whatling, West Des Moines, IA

My family loves this grilled sandwich. I make it for dinner once a week! Sometimes I add some mild Cheddar cheese instead of the peanut butter.

8 slices applewood smoked bacon
8 slices whole-grain bread
1/4 c. peach preserves
1 to 2 apples, cored and thinly sliced
1/4 c. creamy peanut butter
2 to 3 T. butter, softened and divided

In a skillet over medium heat, cook bacon until crisp; drain bacon on paper towels. Spread 4 slices of bread with preserves; layer apple and bacon slices over preserves. Spread remaining bread slices with peanut butter; close sandwiches. Spread tops of sandwiches with half of butter. Place sandwiches butter-side down on a griddle over medium heat. Spread remaining butter on unbuttered side of sandwiches. Cook 2 to 3 minutes per side, until bread is toasted and sandwiches are heated through. Serve warm. Makes 4 sandwiches.

Ranch BLT Wraps

Rachel Dingler, Howell, MI

Our family loves to enjoy these wraps with a bowl of soup.

6 leaves green leaf lettuce
6 sandwich wraps
12-oz. pkg. bacon, crisply cooked
1 lb. boneless, skinless chicken breasts, cooked and cubed
2 tomatoes, diced
ranch salad dressing to taste

Place one leaf lettuce on each sandwich wrap. Top with 2 to 3 slices bacon. Spoon chicken and tomatoes evenly over bacon. Drizzle with salad dressing and roll up. Makes 6.

Peanut Butter Apple-Bacon Sandwich

Ranch BLT Wraps

Skinny Salsa Joes

Skinny Salsa Joes

Marcia Frahm, Urbandale, IA

The longer the beef simmers, the better these taste. Serve the mixture on toasty sandwich buns.

1 lb. ground beef, browned and drained
1/2 c. salsa
8-oz. can tomato sauce
1 T. brown sugar, packed
4 sandwich buns, split

Combine all ingredients in a saucepan except buns; bring to a boil. Reduce heat; simmer 10 to 15 minutes. Serve on buns. Serves 4.

French Bread Pizza Burgers

Christine Gordon, Rapid City, SD

A quick and easy dinner...kids will love to eat this as much as they'll love helping Mom make it! Change it up any way you like, adding other pizza toppings to your own taste.

1 loaf French bread, halved lengthwise
15-oz. can pizza sauce
1 lb. ground pork sausage, browned and drained
3-1/2 oz. pkg. sliced pepperoni
8-oz. pkg. shredded mozzarella cheese

Place both halves of loaf on an ungreased baking sheet, cut sides up. Spread with pizza sauce; top with sausage, pepperoni and cheese. Bake at 350 degrees for 15 minutes or until cheese is melted. Slice to serve. Serves 6 to 8.

French Bread Pizza Burgers

Go-To Slow-Cooker Suppers

(sit back and relax)

Isn't it wonderful to come home to the aroma of an already prepared meal? Let your slow cooker treat you! Try a simmering (and beautiful) Butternut Squash Soup. Serve with a slice of whole-grain bread and your meal is complete. Apple-Stuffed Turkey Breast is easy to prepare in the slow cooker and looks so festive. Chicago Italian Beef benefits from a long, slow simmer to blend the flavors so deliciously. No matter what you choose to make, these easy-to-make recipes are oh-so-good!

Slow-Cooker
Ham & Broccoli Meal-in-One

Hope Davenport, Portland, TX

This tasty rice casserole cooks up while you are away...a truly trouble-free meal!

1 c. long-cooking rice, cooked
16-oz. jar pasteurized process cheese sauce
2 10-3/4 oz. cans cream of chicken soup
2 16-oz. pkgs. frozen chopped broccoli, thawed
salt and pepper to taste
1 lb. cooked ham, cubed

Combine all ingredients in a slow cooker except ham. Cover and cook on low setting for 3-1/2 hours. Add ham and mix well. Cover and cook for an additional 15 to 30 minutes. Serves 6 to 8.

Slow-Cooker Chicken Cacciatore

Barbara Spilsbury, Hacienda Heights, CA

Top hot spaghetti with this delicious dish.

6 boneless, skinless chicken breasts
28-oz. jar spaghetti sauce
2 green peppers, chopped
1 onion, minced
2 T. minced garlic

Place chicken in a slow cooker; top with remaining ingredients. Cover; cook on low setting for 7 to 9 hours. Serves 6.

Apple Spice Country Ribs

Tammi Miller, Attleboro, MA

2 to 3 lbs. boneless country pork ribs
3 baking apples, cored and cut into wedges
1 onion, thinly sliced
2/3 c. apple cider
1 t. cinnamon
1 t. allspice
1/2 t. salt
1/4 t. pepper

Place all ingredients in a 5-quart slow cooker; stir to coat. Cover and cook on low setting for 7 to 9 hours. Juices will thicken as they cool; stir if separated. Serve with mashed potatoes or hot cooked rice if desired. (If bone-in ribs are used, slice into serving-size portions.) Serves 6.

One fall weekend after apple picking, I tossed together this recipe. I was trying to work apples into everything I could think of to use them up, and I used some of the last ones in this slow-cooker recipe. Once it was done, I wished I'd made it first so I could make it again. —Tammi

Apple Spice Country Ribs

Chicago Italian Beef

Chicago Italian Beef

Heather Porter, Villa Park, IL

If you come from Chicago you know Italian beef. Serve with chewy, delicious Italian rolls and top with some of the gravy from the slow cooker...the taste is out of this world!

4 to 5-lb. beef rump roast or bottom round roast
16-oz. jar pepperoncini
16-oz. jar mild giardiniera mix in oil
14-oz. can beef broth
1.05-oz. pkg. Italian salad dressing mix
10 to 14 Italian rolls, split

Place roast in a large slow cooker. Top with undrained pepperoncini and giardeniera; pour in broth and sprinkle with dressing mix. Cover and cook on low setting for 6 to 8 hours. Reserving liquid in slow cooker, shred beef with 2 forks. To serve, top rolls with beef and some of the liquid and vegetables from slow cooker. Serves 10 to 14.

Easy Slow-Cooker Beef Stew

Christy Neubert, O'Fallon, IL

My sister, Crystal, gave me this wonderful recipe. It's so yummy and easy, all you need is fruit and warm bread to make a meal.

1-1/2 lbs. stew beef, cubed
8-oz. pkg. baby carrots
3 to 4 potatoes, cubed
10-3/4 oz. can tomato soup
10-3/4 oz. can beef broth
10-3/4 oz. can French onion soup

Place beef in bottom of a slow cooker sprayed with non-stick vegetable spray. Arrange carrots and potatoes over beef. Combine soups and pour over vegetables. Cover; cook on low setting for 8 to 10 hours or high setting for 6 hours. Serves 3 to 4.

Country Cabin Potatoes

Country Cabin Potatoes

Carol Lytle, Columbus, OH

One fall, we stayed in a beautiful 1800s log cabin in southern Ohio. Not only was it peaceful and relaxing, but the meals they served were wonderful! I got this recipe there.

4 14-1/2 oz. cans sliced potatoes, drained
2 10-3/4 oz. cans cream of celery soup
16-oz. container sour cream
10 slices bacon, crisply cooked and crumbled
6 green onions, thinly sliced

Place potatoes in a slow cooker. In a bowl, combine remaining ingredients; pour over potatoes and stir gently. Cover and cook on high setting for 4 to 5 hours. Makes 10 to 12 servings.

Company Chicken & Stuffing

Amy Blanchard, Hazel Park, MI

Try Cheddar or brick cheese for a tasty flavor change.

4 boneless, skinless chicken breasts
4 slices Swiss cheese
1 pkg. chicken-flavored stuffing mix
2 10-3/4 oz. cans cream of chicken soup
1/2 c. chicken broth

Arrange chicken in a slow cooker; top each piece with a slice of cheese. Mix together stuffing mix, soup and broth; pour into slow cooker. Cover and cook on low setting for 6 to 8 hours. Serves 4.

Poppy Seed Chicken

Don't be tempted to sprinkle on the cracker-crumb mixture while the chicken is in the slow cooker…condensation will make the topping soggy.

6 boneless, skinless chicken breasts
2 10-3/4 oz. cans cream of chicken soup
1 c. milk
1 T. poppy seed
36 round buttery crackers, crushed
1/4 c. butter, melted

Place chicken in a lightly greased slow cooker. Whisk together soup, milk and poppy seed in a medium bowl; pour over chicken. Cover and cook on high setting for one hour. Reduce heat to low setting and cook, covered, 3 hours. Combine cracker crumbs and butter in a bowl, stirring until crumbs are moistened. Sprinkle over chicken just before serving. Serves 6.

Slow-Cooker Butternut Squash Soup

Just chop a few ingredients and combine in the slow cooker for a delicious gourmet soup….so easy!

2-1/2 lbs. butternut squash, peeled, halved, seeded and cubed
2 c. leeks, chopped
2 Granny Smith apples, peeled, cored and diced
2 14-1/2 oz. cans chicken broth
1 c. water
seasoned salt and white pepper to taste
Garnish: freshly ground nutmeg and sour cream

Combine squash, leeks, apples, broth and water in a 4-quart slow cooker. Cover and cook on high setting for 4 hours or until squash and leeks are tender. Carefully purée the hot soup in 3 or 4 batches in a food processor or blender until smooth. Add seasoned salt and white pepper. Garnish with nutmeg and sour cream. Serves 8.

Quick tip

Sometimes a recipe will use only half an onion. Rub the cut side of the remaining half with a little vegetable oil and pop it into a plastic zipping bag…it will stay fresh in the refrigerator for weeks.

Slow-Cooker Butternut Squash Soup

Slow-Cooked Pulled Pork

Heat oil in a skillet over medium heat. Add roast and brown on all sides; remove to a large slow cooker and set aside. Mix soup, catsup and vinegar. Add brown sugar if using; pour over roast. Cover and cook on low setting for 8 to 10 hours, until roast is fork-tender. Remove roast to a platter; discard string and let stand for 10 minutes. Shred roast, using 2 forks; return to slow cooker and stir. Spoon meat and sauce onto bread slices or rolls. Makes 12 sandwiches.

Slow-Cooker Swiss Steak

Lisa Ludwig, Fort Wayne, IN

Your family will love this flavorful version of an old favorite. Pick up a container of heat & eat mashed potatoes for an easy side.

2-lb. beef chuck roast, cut into serving-size pieces
3/4 c. all-purpose flour, divided
2 to 3 T. oil
16-oz. can diced tomatoes
1 onion, sliced
1 T. browning and seasoning sauce

Coat beef with 1/2 cup flour; sauté in oil in a skillet until browned. Arrange beef in a slow cooker. Combine remaining ingredients except remaining flour and pour over beef; cover and cook on low setting for 6 to 8 hours. Slowly stir in remaining flour to make gravy, adding water if necessary. Cook on high setting for 15 minutes, until thickened. Serves 4.

Slow-Cooked Pulled Pork

Tina Goodpasture, Meadowview, VA

A southern-style sandwich favorite! Enjoy it like we do, served with coleslaw and dill pickles.

1 T. oil
3-1/2 to 4-lb. boneless pork shoulder roast, tied
10-1/2 oz. can French onion soup
1 c. catsup
1/4 c. cider vinegar
Optional: 2 T. brown sugar, packed
bread slices or rolls

Tammy's Italian Chicken

Julie Klum, Lake Oswego, OR

2-1/2 lbs. frozen chicken breasts
1-1/2 oz. pkg. spaghetti sauce mix
14-1/2 oz. can diced tomatoes
8-oz. can tomato sauce
cooked penne pasta
Garnish: grated Parmesan cheese

Arrange frozen chicken in a slow cooker. Sprinkle with sauce mix; add tomatoes and tomato sauce. Cover and cook on low setting for 7 to 8 hours, or on high setting for 3-1/2 to 4-1/2 hours. Serve over penne pasta, sprinkled with Parmesan cheese. Makes 4 to 6 servings.

Everyone loves this quick & easy dish! My son gets a thumbs-up from the other firefighters on his crew when it's his turn to cook, and my sister-in-law got rave reviews when she served it to her son's high school football team. —Julie

Tammy's Italian Chicken

Crock O' Brats

Brown bratwurst in a large skillet over medium heat; reserve drippings. Slice bratwurst into one-inch pieces; set aside. Combine remaining ingredients in a slow cooker. Stir in bratwurst slices with pan drippings. Cover and cook on high setting for 4 to 6 hours, or until potatoes are tender. Serves 6.

Apple-Stuffed Turkey Breast

Dale Duncan, Waterloo, IA

1-1/2 c. long-grain & wild rice, uncooked
2 apples, peeled, cored and chopped
1 onion, finely chopped
1/2 c. sweetened dried cranberries
3 c. water
4 to 5-lb. boneless, skinless turkey breast

Combine rice, apples, onion and cranberries in a slow cooker; pour water over top. Mix well. Place turkey on top of rice mixture. Cover and cook on low setting for 8 to 9 hours. Serves 10.

Crock O' Brats

Naomi Cooper, Delaware, OH

Serve with hearty rye bread and homestyle applesauce sprinkled with cinnamon.

20-oz. pkg. bratwurst
5 potatoes, peeled and cubed
1 tart apple, cored and cubed
1 onion, chopped
1/4 c. brown sugar, packed
27-oz. can sauerkraut, drained

The combination of wild rice, apples and cranberries really gives this turkey an amazing flavor. The slow cooker helps the flavors blend so nicely. —Dale

Apple-Stuffed Turkey Breast

Dan's Broccoli & Cheese Soup

Dan's Broccoli & Cheese Soup

Serve this rich and creamy soup with a slice of marble bread and fresh fruit for a complete meal.

16-oz. pkg. frozen chopped broccoli, thawed
10-3/4 oz. cream of mushroom soup
1 c. milk
1 c. half-and-half
8-oz. pkg. cream cheese, cubed
1/2 c. pasteurized process cheese spread, cubed
salt and pepper to taste

Combine all ingredients in a slow cooker. Cover and cook on high setting for 30 to 40 minutes. Reduce to low setting; cover and cook for an additional 3 to 4 hours, stirring occasionally. Serves 6

Quick tip

Make it simple by using a slow cooker for dishes that you would normally cook on the stove. Try stews, chili or even chicken and noodles. It cooks by itself, leaving you more time for family & friends.

Joan's Chicken Stuffing Casserole

Joan Brochu, Harwick, PA

Hearty and filling, this chicken dish will be the first to disappear at any potluck.

2 6-oz. pkgs. chicken-flavored stuffing mix
2 10-3/4 oz. cans cream of chicken soup, divided
1/2 c. milk
3 c. cooked chicken, cubed
8-oz. pkg. shredded Cheddar cheese

Prepare stuffing mix according to package directions; place in a lightly greased 5-quart slow cooker. Stir in one can soup. Stir together remaining soup, milk and chicken in a separate bowl. Add to slow cooker. Sprinkle cheese over top. Cover and cook on high setting for 3 hours or on low setting for 4 to 6 hours. Serves 6.

Easy Slow-Cooker Steak

Ashley Whitehead, Sidney, TX

Like lots of gravy? Use two envelopes of soup mix and two cans of soup.

2 to 2-1/2 lb. beef round steak
1-1/2 oz. pkg. onion soup mix
1/4 c. water
10-3/4 oz. can cream of mushroom soup

Slice steak into 5 serving-size pieces; place in a slow cooker. Add soup mix, water and soup. Cover and cook on low setting for 6 to 8 hours. Makes 5 servings.

Melt-in-Your-Mouth Pork Chops

Renee Spec, Crescent, PA

An easy, economical slow-cooker meal that's very tasty. My husband is happy to take any leftovers for his lunch.

4 pork loin chops
10-3/4 oz. can cream of celery soup
1-1/3 c. water
garlic salt and dried parsley to taste
cooked rice

Place pork chops in a slow cooker. Blend together soup, water and seasonings; spoon over pork chops. Cover and cook on low setting for 6 to 8 hours, or until pork is cooked through. Serve chops and gravy over cooked rice. Makes 4 servings.

Mom's Slow-Cooker Mini Reubens

Cheryl Breeden, North Platte, NE

1/4 to 1/2 lb. deli corned beef, chopped
2 16-oz. pkgs. shredded Swiss cheese
8-oz. bottle Thousand Island salad dressing
32-oz. pkg. refrigerated sauerkraut, drained and chopped
Optional: 1 t. caraway seed
1 to 2 loaves party rye bread
Garnish: dill pickle slices

Put all ingredients except party rye and pickles in a slow cooker. Cover and cook on low setting for about 4 hours, or until mixture is hot and cheese is melted. Stir to blend well. To serve, arrange party rye slices and pickles on separate plates around slow cooker. Makes 10 to 12 servings.

This was always my mom's favorite recipe during football season. Add a fresh fruit salad and some homemade cookies to make the meal complete. Even if your team loses, dinner will be a winner! —Cheryl

Melt-in-Your-Mouth Pork Chops

Mom's Slow-Cooker Mini Reubens

Swiss Steak

Jean Carter, Rockledge, FL

*I have served this for years to a variety of very picky eaters…
they all loved it! Buttery mashed potatoes are delicious
alongside.*

2 lbs. boneless beef round steak, cut into 6 serving pieces
1.1-oz. pkg. beefy onion soup mix
3 c. onion, sliced
28-oz. can diced tomatoes
3 T. all-purpose flour
1 c. water

Arrange steak in a slow cooker. Sprinkle soup mix
over steak; arrange onion slices all around. Top with
tomatoes. Cover and cook on low setting for 8 hours, or
on high setting for 6 hours. Remove steak and vegetables
from slow cooker; set aside. Mix together flour and
water; add to slow cooker and stir until thickened. Spoon
gravy over steak to serve. Makes 4 to 6 servings.

Tangy Pork Ribs

Jo Ann

*Thick, country-style ribs are always a family favorite…now this
is the only way I serve them.*

1/4 c. soy sauce
1/3 c. orange marmalade
3 T. catsup
2 cloves garlic, minced
3 to 4 lbs. country-style pork ribs

Combine soy sauce, marmalade, catsup and garlic in a
small bowl. Pour half into a slow cooker; top with ribs
and drizzle with remaining sauce. Cover and cook on low
setting for 6 hours, or until tender. Serves 6 to 8.

Savory Herb Roast

Karla Neese, Edmond, OK

3-lb. boneless beef chuck roast
salt and pepper to taste
1 to 2 T. oil
1 T. fresh chives, chopped
1 T. fresh parsley, chopped
1 T. fresh basil, chopped
1 c. beef broth
Optional: 4 to 6 potatoes, peeled and quartered;
  3 to 4 carrots, peeled and cut into chunks

Sprinkle roast generously with salt and pepper. Heat oil
in a skillet; add herbs. Brown roast on all sides. Place in
slow cooker; add broth. Cover and cook on low setting
for 6 to 8 hours. Add potatoes and carrots during the last
2 hours of cooking if desired. Serves 6.

*My mom would always put this
roast into the slow cooker early
on Sunday mornings, before
getting ready for church. When we
came home from church around
noon, the whole house smelled
wonderful! Now I make it for a
special weeknight dinner! —Karla*

Savory Herb Roast

Pepperoni-Pizza Rigatoni

Pepperoni-Pizza Rigatoni

JoAnn

Personalize this recipe by adding mushrooms, black olives or any of your family's other favorite pizza toppings.

1-1/2 lbs. ground beef, browned and drained
8-oz. pkg. rigatoni, cooked
16-oz. pkg. shredded mozzarella cheese
10-3/4 oz. can cream of tomato soup
2 14-oz. jars pizza sauce
8-oz. pkg. sliced pepperoni

Alternate layers of ground beef, cooked rigatoni, cheese, soup, sauce and pepperoni in a slow cooker. Cover and cook on low setting for 4 hours. Serves 6.

Mexican Chicken Chili

Beth Smith, Manchester, MI

My sister-in-law Penny made this slow-cooker stew for a gathering and it has become my son Nathan's favorite soup.

3 to 4 boneless, skinless chicken breasts
2 15-oz. cans Great Northern beans, drained
15-oz. can hominy, drained
4-oz. can chopped green chiles
10-3/4 oz. can low-sodium cream of mushroom soup
1-1/4 oz. pkg. taco seasoning mix
Optional: milk or chicken broth
Garnish: nacho cheese-flavored tortilla chips

Place chicken in a 4-quart slow cooker. Layer with beans, hominy, chiles and soup; sprinkle taco seasoning over top. Cover and cook on low setting for 7 to 8 hours. Do not peek and do not stir during cooking. At serving time, use a spoon to break up chicken; stir. If chili is too thick, add a little milk or broth to desired consistency. Serve with tortilla chips. Makes 6 servings.

Mexican Chicken Chili

Lemony "Baked" Chicken

This yummy chicken just falls off the bones and is tender and juicy every time!

3 to 4-lb. roasting chicken
2 T. olive oil
1 lemon, cut in half
2 cloves garlic, minced
1 t. dried parsley
salt and pepper to taste

Pat chicken dry with a paper towel; rub with oil. Put lemon inside chicken; place in a slow cooker. Sprinkle with seasonings. Cover and cook on high setting for one hour. Turn to low setting and cook an additional 6 to 7 hours. Makes 4 servings.

Quick tip

Fresh herbs may lose flavor after hours of slow cooking. Stir them in near the end of the cooking time or check and add a little more seasoning just before serving.

Smoky Hobo Dinner

Julie Pak, Henryetta, OK

Away from home all day? This slow-cooker creation will have dinner waiting for you!

5 potatoes, peeled and quartered
1 head cabbage, coarsely chopped into bite-size pieces
16-oz. pkg. baby carrots
1 onion, thickly sliced into wedges
salt and pepper to taste
14-oz. pkg. smoked pork sausage, sliced into 2-inch pieces
1/2 c. water
Garnish: fresh parsley

Spray a 5 to 6-quart slow cooker with non-stick vegetable spray. Layer vegetables, sprinkling each layer with salt and pepper. Place sausage on top. Pour water down one side of slow cooker. Cover and cook on low setting for 6 to 8 hours. Serves 6.

Yummy Ham Sandwiches

This simple recipe is sure to become one of your favorite slow-cooker suppers.

6-lb. bone-in ham
8-oz. jar mustard
16-oz. pkg. brown sugar, packed
24 dinner rolls, split

Place ham in a large slow cooker; cover with water. Cover and cook on low setting for 8 to 10 hours, until ham is very tender. Drain; let cool. Shred ham and return to slow cooker; stir in mustard and brown sugar. Cover and cook on low setting just until heated through. Serve on rolls. Makes 24 mini-sandwiches.

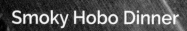
Smoky Hobo Dinner

Nana's Easy Pot Roast

Natalie Anstine, Canton, OH

This is my mother-in-law's slow-cooker roast. It's scrumptious...and I was shocked at how simple it is to make! Everyone in the family asks her to make this dish for their birthday meal. The soup and onion make a perfect gravy without having to add anything else!

2 to 3-lb. beef chuck roast
10-3/4 oz. can golden mushroom soup
1 sweet onion, thinly sliced

Place roast in a slow cooker. Pour soup over roast; top with onion slices. Cover and cook on low setting for 5 to 6 hours, until roast is tender. Serve with gravy from slow cooker. Makes 6 to 8 servings.

Newlywed Beef & Noodles

Shannon Kennedy, Delaware, OH

I was just recently married and this is one of my first original recipes.

1 lb. stew beef, cubed and browned
3 14-1/2 oz. cans beef broth
4-1/2 c. water
3 to 4 cubes beef bouillon
8-oz. pkg. egg noodles, uncooked

Add beef, broth and water to a slow cooker; stir in bouillon cubes. Cover and cook on low to medium setting for 4 to 6 hours; add noodles. Cover and cook on low setting until noodles are done. Serves 4.

Hot Chicken Slow-Cooker Sandwiches

Brenda Smith, Monroe, IN

28-oz. can cooked chicken
2 10-3/4 oz. cans cream of chicken soup
4 T. grated Parmesan cheese
7 slices bread, toasted and cubed
1/4 c. sweet red pepper, chopped
24 dinner rolls, split

In a large bowl combine all ingredients, except dinner rolls, and pour into a 5-quart slow-cooker. Cover and cook on low setting for 3 hours. Serve on rolls. Makes 24 mini-sandwiches.

Can't decide what to have for dinner? Sandwiches in the slow cooker! What could be easier? And the creaminess of the chicken makes this a family-favorite meal! —Brenda

Hot Chicken Slow-Cooker Sandwiches

Glazed Corned Beef

Claire Bertram, Lexington, KY

This brisket simmers all day in the slow cooker until it is fork-tender. Baste it before you serve...so simple!

4 to 5-lb. corned beef brisket
2-1/2 T. mustard
2 t. prepared horseradish
2 T. red wine vinegar
1/4 c. honey

In a 5-quart slow cooker, cover brisket with water. Cover and cook on low setting for 10 to 12 hours or until tender. Place corned beef in an ungreased 13"x9" baking pan. In a small bowl, combine mustard, horseradish, vinegar and honey; baste beef. Bake, uncovered, at 400 degrees for 20 minutes or until brisket browns; baste occasionally. Serves 10 to 14.

County Fair Italian Sausages

Dale Duncan, Waterloo, IA

19.76-oz. pkg. Italian pork sausages
1 green pepper, sliced
1 onion, sliced
26-oz. jar pasta sauce
5 hoagie rolls, split
5 slices provolone cheese

Brown sausages in a non-stick skillet over medium heat; place in a 4-quart slow cooker. Add pepper and onion; cover with pasta sauce. Cover slow cooker and cook on low setting for 4 to 6 hours. Place sausages in rolls; top with sauce mixture and cheese. Makes 5 sandwiches.

Slow-Cooker Country Chicken & Dumplings

Joanne Curran, Arlington, MA

4 boneless, skinless chicken breasts, cut up and browned
2 10-3/4 oz. cans cream of chicken soup
2 T. butter, sliced
1 onion, finely diced
1 c. frozen peas
2 7-1/2 oz. tubes refrigerated biscuits, torn
Garnish: chopped parsley

Place chicken, soup, butter and onion in a 4-quart slow cooker; add enough water to cover chicken. Cover and cook on high setting for 4 hours. Add peas and biscuits to slow cooker; gently push biscuits into cooking liquid. Cover and continue cooking for about 1-1/2 hours, until biscuits are done in the center. Serve with a garnish of chopped parsley. Serves 6.

Everyone loves chicken and dumplings! Using refrigerated biscuits for the dumplings and a slow cooker to heat makes this recipe a lifesaver on busy weeknights. —Joanne

Slow-Cooker Country Chicken & Dumplings

Slow-Cooker Rich Beef Stew

Slow-Cooker Rich Beef Stew

Jennifer Levy, Warners, NY

2-1/2 lbs. stew beef, cubed
10-3/4 oz. can cream of mushroom soup
10-3/4 oz. can French onion soup
1 c. dry red wine or beef broth
1 c. fresh mushrooms, sliced
cooked egg noodles

Combine all ingredients except noodles in a slow cooker. Stir to mix. Cover and cook on low setting for 8 to 10 hours. Serve over cooked egg noodles. Serves 6.

This recipe was given to me by my sister, Karen. We both make it often for family meals, and we're proud to serve it to company too! It's delicious... even our picky kids eat it and ask for seconds. Serve with crusty bread to enjoy all the scrumptious gravy. —Jennifer

Lazy Pierogie Casserole

Kelly Alderson, Erie, PA

Serve with grilled sausages...yum!

8-oz. pkg. bowtie pasta, cooked
4 to 6 potatoes, peeled and sliced 1/2-inch thick
2 8-oz. pkgs. shredded Cheddar cheese
3/4 c. butter, sliced
3/4 c. bacon, crisply cooked and crumbled
1 c. onion, finely chopped
salt and pepper to taste

Layer bowties and remaining ingredients in a slow cooker. Cover and cook on low setting for 7 to 8 hours. Stir gently before serving. Makes 4 to 6 servings.

Pork Chops à la Orange

Rogene Rogers, Bemidji, MN

These pork chops have the taste of a tropical luau, and they're made so easily in the slow cooker!

3 lbs. pork chops
salt and pepper to taste
2 c. orange juice
2 11-oz. cans mandarin oranges, drained
8-oz. can pineapple tidbits, drained
cooked egg noodles

Sprinkle pork chops with salt and pepper; place in a slow cooker. Pour orange juice over pork. Cover and cook on low setting for 6 to 8 hours or on high setting for 3 to 4 hours. About 30 minutes before serving, add oranges and pineapple; cover and continue cooking just until warm. Serve with cooked noodles. Serves 6 to 8.

Slow-Cooker Smoked Sausage Stew

Susie Gray, Winchester, IN

Bake a pan of cornbread to serve alongside this filling stew.

4 to 5 potatoes, peeled and cubed
2 16-oz. cans green beans
1-lb. pkg. smoked sausage, sliced
1 onion, chopped
2 T. butter, sliced

Layer potatoes, green beans, sausage and onion in a slow cooker; dot with butter. Cover and cook on low setting for 4 to 5 hours. Serves 6.

Elizabeth's Slow-Cooker White Chili

Elizabeth Tipton, Knoxville, TN

Garnish with crushed white-corn tortilla chips...a clever use for those broken chips that linger at the bottom of the bag!

1 lb. boneless, skinless chicken breasts, cooked and shredded
4 15.8-oz. cans Great Northern beans
16-oz. jar salsa
8-oz. pkg. shredded Pepper Jack cheese
2 t. ground cumin
1/2 c. chicken broth
Optional: 12-oz. can beer or 1-1/2 c. chicken broth

Combine all ingredients except optional beer or broth in a 5-quart slow cooker. Add beer or broth for a thinner consistency, if desired. Cover and cook on low setting for 4 hours, or until heated through. Serves 6 to 8.

Zesty Picante Chicken

Sonya Collett, Sioux City, IA

4 boneless, skinless chicken breasts, browned
16-oz. jar picante sauce
15-1/2 oz. can black beans, drained and rinsed
4 slices Cheddar cheese
2-1/4 c. cooked rice
Optional: sliced green onions

Place chicken in a 5-quart slow cooker; add picante sauce. Spread black beans over the top. Cover and cook on high setting for 3 hours or until juices run clear when chicken is pierced with a fork. Top with cheese slices; cover and cook until melted. Spoon over rice to serve. Garnish with green onions, if desired. Serves 4.

Spice up suppertime with yummy southwestern-style chicken breasts...made in the slow cooker! Cheese and picante sauce combine for a zesty and flavorful tang and the black beans add great texture. —Sonya

Zesty Picante Chicken

Chicken Artichoke Pasta

Slow-Cooker Beefy Taco Soup

Chicken Artichoke Pasta

A simple jar of Alfredo sauce and artichokes make this dish an easy and delicious weeknight favorite!

16-oz. pkg. frozen grilled chicken breast strips
1 T. chicken bouillon granules
1/4 c. water
17-oz. jar Alfredo sauce
6-1/2 oz. jar marinated artichoke hearts, drained
6-oz. pkg. angel hair pasta, cooked
Optional: chopped parsley

Place chicken strips in a slow cooker with bouillon and water. Cover and cook on low setting for 2 to 3 hours. Stir in sauce and artichokes; turn slow cooker to high setting and cook an additional 30 minutes. Serve over prepared pasta. Serves 4.

Slow-Cooker Beefy Taco Soup

Erin McRae, Beaverton, OR

Top each bowl of this hearty soup with feta cheese and serve with taco chips. Yum!

1 lb. ground beef, browned
15-oz. can stewed tomatoes
15-oz. can kidney beans, drained and rinsed
1-1/4 oz. env. taco seasoning mix
8-oz. can tomato sauce
Optional: feta cheese

Stir together all ingredients; pour into a 3 to 4-quart slow cooker. Cover and cook on low setting for 6 to 8 hours; stir occasionally. Serves 4 to 6.

Slow-Cooker Sauerkraut Pork Roast

Teresa McBee, Billings, MT

Just add mashed potatoes...everyone will beg for seconds!

3 to 4-lb. pork roast
1 T. oil
salt and pepper to taste
15-oz. can sauerkraut

Brown pork roast on all sides in oil in a skillet over high heat. Sprinkle with salt and pepper. Place roast in a 5-quart slow cooker; top with sauerkraut. Cover and cook on low setting for 6 to 8 hours. Serves 6 to 8.

Slow-Cooker Sauerkraut Pork Roast

Easiest-Ever Turkey Dinner

Claire Bertram, Lexington, KY

What a wonderful dinner for a small gathering! So easy and delicious!

3 potatoes, peeled and cubed
3 skinless turkey thighs
12-oz. jar homestyle turkey gravy
1 t. dried parsley
1/2 t. dried thyme
1/8 t. pepper

Arrange potatoes in a slow cooker; place turkey on top. Stir together gravy and seasonings in a bowl; pour over turkey. Cover and cook on low setting for 8 to 10 hours, until juices run clear when turkey is pierced. Remove turkey and potatoes from slow cooker using a slotted spoon. Stir gravy and serve with turkey. Serves 6.

Down-Home Split Pea Soup

Jude Trimnal, Brevard, NC

Let this comfort-food split pea soup simmer in the slow cooker all afternoon.

8 c. water
2 c. dried split peas, sorted and rinsed
1-1/2 c. celery, sliced
1-1/2 c. carrot, peeled and sliced
1 onion, sliced
salt and pepper to taste
1 to 2 c. cooked ham, cubed

Combine all ingredients in a 4-quart slow cooker. Cover and cook on low for 4 to 6 hours. Serves 8 to 10.

Down-Home Split Pea Soup

Lemon-Poppy Seed Cake

Lemon-Poppy Seed Cake

Rogene Rogers, Bemidji, MN

15.8-oz. lemon-poppy seed bread mix
1 egg, beaten
8-oz. container sour cream
1-1/4 c. water, divided
1/2 c. sugar
1/4 c. lemon juice

Combine bread mix, egg, sour cream and 1/2 cup water in a bowl. Stir until well-moistened; spread in a lightly greased 3 to 4-quart slow cooker. Combine 3/4 cup water and remaining ingredients in a small saucepan; bring to a boil. Pour boiling mixture over batter in slow cooker. Cover and cook on high setting for 2 to 2-1/2 hours, until edges are golden. Turn off slow cooker; let cake cool in slow cooker for 30 minutes with lid ajar. When cool enough to handle, hold a large plate over top of slow cooker and invert to turn out cake. Serves 10 to 12.

Peachy Good Dessert

Tina Schroer, Jefferson City, MO

My husband and children just love this dessert! If there's any left, it's yummy over ice cream.

1/3 c. biscuit baking mix
2/3 c. quick-cooking oats, uncooked
1/2 c. sugar
1/2 c. brown sugar, packed
1/2 t. cinnamon
4 c. peaches, peeled, pitted and sliced

Mix dry ingredients together. Toss with peaches and pour into a slow cooker that has been sprayed with non-stick vegetable spray. Cover and cook on low setting for 4 to 6 hours. Makes 6 to 8 servings.

Tahitian Rice Pudding

Beth Kramer, Port Saint Lucie, FL

3/4 c. long-cooking rice, uncooked
15-oz. can cream of coconut
12-oz. can evaporated milk
2-3/4 c. water
Optional: 1 T. dark rum
2/3 c. sweetened flaked coconut

Stir together rice, cream, milk and water in a 3 to 4-quart slow cooker until combined. Cover and cook on low setting for 4 to 5 hours. Remove crock from slow cooker. Stir in rum, if desired. Let pudding cool for 10 minutes. Heat a small non-stick skillet over medium heat. Add coconut; cook and stir for 4 to 5 minutes, until toasted. Remove coconut and set aside. Spoon pudding into dessert bowls; sprinkle with toasted coconut. Serves 6 to 8.

Simmered Autumn Applesauce

Jennifer Levy, Warners, NY

The kids will love this recipe! It's perfect for the apples you picked together at the orchard. Let the delicious aroma from your slow cooker fill your kitchen on a crisp fall day.

8 apples, several different varieties, peeled, cored
   and cubed
1 c. water
1/2 c. brown sugar, packed
1 t. cinnamon
1/2 t. pumpkin pie spice

Add all ingredients to a 3 to 4-quart slow cooker; stir. Cover and cook on low setting for 6 to 8 hours. Mash apples with the back of a spoon; stir again. Let cool slightly before serving. Serves 6.

Midweek Meatless Main Dishes

(quick vegetarian recipes)

Look no further for some meatless recipes made with just a handful of ingredients. Melinda's Veggie Stir-Fry will serve up great nutrition as well as great taste! You'll find plenty of protein in a California Omelet…serve with toast and fresh fruit for a satisfying meatless meal. Feel like making sandwiches tonight? Grill Irene's Portabella Burgers for a meatless version of a great burger. Your entire family will love these tasty dishes and no one will miss the meat!

Summertime Tomato Tart

Linda Belon, Wintersville, OH

Use your abundance of vine-ripe tomatoes in this yummy, summery treat.

4 tomatoes, sliced
9-inch pie crust
8-oz. pkg shredded mozzarella cheese
2 T. fresh basil, chopped
1/4 c. olive oil

Arrange tomato slices in bottom of pie crust. Sprinkle evenly with cheese and basil; drizzle with oil. Bake at 400 degrees for 30 minutes. Let stand for 5 minutes before slicing. Serves 6.

Mom's Sweet Apple Omelet

Kristy Markners, Fort Mill, SC

This is a recipe my mom has been making as long as I can remember. My brother and I used to fight over who could eat the last serving...it's that good!

4 c. applesauce
3 eggs, beaten
1 c. sugar
1 T. cinnamon
Optional: 1 to 1-1/2 T. flour

Whisk together all ingredients, adding flour if applesauce is very runny. Pour into an ungreased 9" pie plate. Bake, uncovered, at 350 degrees for one hour, or until center is firm. Scoop and serve warm. Makes 8 servings.

California Omelet

Not just for breakfast, omelets make the quickest and tastiest dinners for the entire family...you can personalize each one to include favorite flavors.

1 T. oil
3 to 4 eggs
1/4 c. milk
salt and pepper to taste
1 avocado, sliced
2 green onions, diced
1/2 c. shredded Monterey jack cheese

Heat oil in a skillet over medium-low heat. Whisk together eggs, milk, salt and pepper in a bowl; pour into skillet. Cook until eggs are lightly golden on bottom and partially set on top. Sprinkle with remaining ingredients; carefully fold omelet in half so toppings are covered. Reduce heat to medium-low and cook, uncovered, about 5 to 10 minutes. Serves 2.

Quick tip

A low bowl or crock looks wonderful filled with avocados and tomatoes. Use it as a centerpiece while they ripen.

California Omelet

No-Crust Spinach Quiche

No-Crust Spinach Quiche

Mary Mayall, Dracut, MA

If you want meat in this dish, add chopped ham or crumbled bacon to this delicious crustless quiche.

10-oz. pkg. frozen chopped spinach, thawed and drained
Optional: 1/2 c. onion or mushrooms, chopped
6 eggs, beaten
1/2 c. milk
1 c. shredded Swiss or Cheddar cheese

Spread spinach in a greased 9" pie plate. Sprinkle onion and/or mushrooms on top, if desired. Beat together eggs and milk; stir in cheese. Pour egg mixture evenly over spinach. Bake at 350 degrees for 25 to 35 minutes, until top is golden and a knife tip inserted into center comes out clean. Cool slightly before cutting. Serves 6.

Cheese & Chive Scrambled Eggs

Goldenrod Eggs

Fawn McKenzie, Wenatchee, WA

This simple dish will become a favorite comfort food as well as a great weeknight dinner.

5 to 6 eggs, hard-boiled, peeled and halved
6 T. butter or sausage drippings
6 T. all-purpose flour
2-3/4 c. to 3 c. milk
salt and pepper to taste
toast or split biscuits

Place egg yolks in a small bowl; mash and set aside. Chop whites and set aside. Place butter or drippings in a medium saucepan over medium-high heat; whisk in flour. Slowly pour in milk until desired consistency is achieved. Continue to heat through until mixture thickens. Stir in egg whites; season with salt and pepper as desired. Spoon over toast or biscuits. Sprinkle mashed egg yolks over each serving. Serves 4.

Cheese & Chive Scrambled Eggs

Deborah Wells, Broken Arrow, OK

Paired with hot biscuits, this makes a great dinner for any night of the week!

6 eggs, beaten
1/4 t. lemon pepper
1 T. fresh chives, chopped
1/8 t. salt
1 T. butter
1/3 c. shredded Colby Jack cheese
1/3 c. cream cheese, softened

In a bowl, combine eggs, pepper, chives and salt; set aside. Melt butter in a skillet over medium-low heat; add egg mixture. Stir to scramble, cooking until set. Remove from heat; stir in cheeses until melted. Serves 2 to 3.

French Onion Tart

Robbi Courtaway, Webster Groves, MO

This is one of my favorite easy main dishes. It's scrumptious and very inexpensive to make. Sweet onions are delicious, but you can use any kind. I've heard that in France street vendors sell these tarts by the slice at room temperature...it's true that leftover slices are amazingly good served cold!

4 to 5 onions, thinly sliced and separated into rings
1-1/2 T. oil, divided
salt and pepper to taste
6-1/2 oz. pkg. pizza crust mix
1 c. shredded Swiss cheese

In a skillet over medium-high heat, sauté onions in one tablespoon oil for about 20 minutes, until light golden and caramelized. Add salt and pepper to taste. Meanwhile, prepare pizza crust mix and let stand several minutes, according to package instructions. Spread out dough in a lightly greased 12" round pizza pan; lightly coat with remaining oil. Spread onions evenly over dough. Sprinkle cheese evenly over onions. Bake on the bottom rack of oven at 425 degrees for 12 to 15 minutes, until edges of crust are golden and cheese is melted and bubbly. Cool slightly; cut into wedges. Serves 3 to 4.

Jolene's Chickpea Medley

Jolene Koval, Thunder Bay, Ontario

15-oz. can garbanzo beans, drained and rinsed
1 red pepper, diced
1 c. kale, finely shredded
1 zucchini, diced
1 ear corn, steamed, kernels cut off, or 1/2 c. frozen
  corn, thawed, steamed and cooled
1/2 c. Italian salad dressing

In a salad bowl, combine beans and vegetables. Drizzle with salad dressing; toss to mix. Let stand 15 minutes before serving to allow flavors to blend. Makes 4 servings.

This unusual meatless salad goes together in a jiffy! The garbanzo beans add protein, texture and amazing flavor. And it is just such a beautiful dish to serve! Add some homemade bread and a favorite cheese and you have a complete meal. —Jolene

Jolene's Chickpea Medley

Egg-Topped Pizza

Egg-Topped Pizza

Connie Hilty, Pearland, TX

Is there anything better than pizza with some meatless protein? Try this and you'll know what I mean!

11-oz. tube refrigerated thin-crust pizza dough
14-oz. can pizza sauce
16-oz. container ricotta cheese
1/4 c. fresh oregano
3 T. sun-dried tomatoes, chopped
4 eggs
salt and pepper to taste

Roll out dough into a 13-inch by 9-inch rectangle; transfer to a greased rimmed baking sheet. Spread pizza sauce on dough, leaving a 1/2-inch border. Top with cheese, oregano and sun-dried tomatoes. Bake at 500 degrees for 4 to 5 minutes, or until crust begins to turn golden. Crack each egg into a small bowl and slip onto pizza, being careful not to break the yolks. Bake for another 5 minutes, until eggs are done as desired. Serves 4.

Mexican Egg Bake

Nadine Watson, Aurora, CO

Refried beans make a perfect side for this dish.

12 corn tortillas, torn
16-oz. can green chili sauce
16-oz. pkg. shredded Cheddar cheese, divided
6 eggs
Garnish: sour cream, shredded lettuce, sliced tomato

Layer tortillas, chili sauce and 3/4 of cheese in an ungreased 13"x9" baking pan. Break eggs over top, spacing evenly. Sprinkle with remaining cheese. Bake, uncovered, at 350 degrees for 30 to 40 minutes. Slice into squares and garnish with sour cream, lettuce and sliced tomato. Serves 8 to 10.

Blueberry Pillows

Blueberry Pillows

Kristie Rigo, Friedens, PA

A delightful blend of cream cheese and blueberries are stuffed inside this French toast.

8-oz. pkg. cream cheese, softened
16 slices Italian bread
1/2 c. blueberries
2 eggs, beaten
1/2 c. milk
1 t. vanilla extract

Spread cream cheese evenly on 8 bread slices; arrange blueberries in a single layer over cream cheese. Top with remaining bread slices, gently pressing to seal; set aside. Whisk together eggs, milk and vanilla in a small bowl; brush over bread slices. Arrange on a greased hot griddle; cook until golden. Flip and cook other side until golden. Serves 8.

Corn Surprise

Corn Surprise

Eva Rae Walter, Paola, KS

A winter warm-up recipe that's easy to double, making it perfect for potlucks.

15-1/4 oz. can corn
8-oz. pkg. small pasta shells, uncooked
16-oz. can cream-style corn
8-oz. pkg. shredded Mexican-blend cheese

Combine undrained corn and remaining ingredients in a bowl. Transfer to a greased 13"x9" baking pan. Bake, covered, at 350 degrees for 45 minutes, or until pasta is tender. As it bakes, stir casserole several times; uncover for the last 10 minutes of cooking. Serves 6 to 8.

Quick tip

Farmers' market foods taste so fresh because they're all grown and picked in season at the peak of flavor...lettuce, asparagus and strawberries in the springtime; tomatoes, peppers and sweet corn in the summer; squash and greens in the fall and winter.

Fried Spaghetti

Tiffany Jones, Locust Grove, AR

My dad and I love Chinese food. I tried spaghetti noodles instead of rice...it turned out to be a favorite!

12-oz. pkg. thin spaghetti, uncooked
3 T. sesame oil
1/2 onion, chopped
1/4 c. frozen peas
2 T. soy sauce
2 T. teriyaki sauce

Cook spaghetti according to package directions; drain. Meanwhile, in a large saucepan, heat oil over medium heat. Sauté onion and frozen peas for 3 minutes, or until onion is soft. Stir in soy sauce, teriyaki sauce and spaghetti. Mix everything well. Cook for 5 minutes, stirring occasionally. Serves 4.

Tortino de Carciofi

Denise Piccirilli, Huber Heights, OH

This simple recipe for a baked artichoke omelet is a traditional Italian dish. We enjoy it very much.

2 T. olive oil
1 c. canned artichoke quarters, drained
4 eggs, beaten
1/2 t. salt

Heat olive oil in a skillet over medium heat. Cook artichokes, stirring frequently, for 8 to 10 minutes, until golden. Spread artichokes in a buttered one-quart casserole dish. Whisk together eggs and salt until frothy; pour over artichokes. Bake, uncovered, at 400 degrees for 15 minutes, or until firm. Cut into wedges; serve immediately. Serves 4.

Savory Italian Pancakes

Johnny Appleseed Toast

Rebekah Spooner, Huntsville, AL

4 slices cinnamon-raisin bread
1-1/2 T. butter, divided
1 Gala apple, cored and sliced
4 t. honey
1 t. cinnamon

Spread each slice of bread with one teaspoon of butter. Cover each bread slice with an apple slice; drizzle with one teaspoon honey and sprinkle with cinnamon. Place topped bread slices on an ungreased baking sheet. Broil on high for one to 2 minutes, until toasted and golden. Makes 4 servings.

Savory Italian Pancakes

Jessica Parker, Mulvane, KS

Give the kids the unexpected for dinner...these will disappear fast!

2 c. biscuit baking mix
1 c. milk
2 eggs, beaten
1/2 c. shredded mozzarella cheese
1/2 c. tomato, chopped
2 t. Italian seasoning
Garnish: pizza sauce, grated Parmesan cheese

Stir together baking mix, milk and eggs until well blended; add remaining ingredients except garnish. Heat a lightly greased griddle over medium-high heat. Ladle batter by 1/4 cupfuls onto the griddle; cook until golden on both sides. Garnish with warmed pizza sauce and Parmesan cheese. Makes 15 pancakes.

I'm a teacher, and we make this every fall to celebrate Johnny Appleseed with our little ones in September. It also makes a wonderfully quick fall dinner when you serve it with Cheddar cheese slices and cold milk. —Rebekah

Johnny Appleseed Toast

Garden-Fresh Pesto Pizza

Jennifer Oglesby, Brookville, IN

With this easy pizza, you can really taste what summer is all about! I came up with this recipe last summer when I had a bounty of cherry tomatoes and fresh basil.

12-inch pizza crust
1/3 to 1/2 c. basil pesto
2 c. shredded mozzarella cheese
1-1/2 c. cherry tomatoes, halved
Optional: 4 leaves fresh basil

Place crust on a 12" pizza pan, lightly greased with non-stick vegetable spray if directed on package. Spread pesto over pizza crust and top with cheese. Scatter tomatoes over cheese; add a basil leaf to each quarter of the pizza, if desired. Bake at 425 degrees for about 8 to 10 minutes, until crust is crisp and cheese is lightly golden. Cut into wedges. Makes 8 servings.

Irene's Portabella Burgers

Irene Robinson, Brookville, IN

Scrumptious...I promise you won't miss the meat! Serve this on pretzel buns to bring out the beauty of the mushrooms. If you don't wish to fire up the grill, use a heavy grill skillet on your stovetop. However you make this amazing sandwich, your family will love it and won't believe the wonderful flavor and texture of this meatless sandwich.

4 portabella mushroom caps
1 c. Italian salad dressing
4 pretzel or sourdough buns, split
4 slices Muenster or Gruyère cheese
Garnish: romaine lettuce or arugula

Combine mushrooms and salad dressing in a plastic zipping bag, turning to coat. Chill 30 minutes, turning occasionally. Remove mushrooms, discarding dressing. Grill mushrooms, covered with grill lid, over medium heat for 2 to 3 minutes on each side. Grill buns, cut-side down, one minute, or until toasted. Top buns with mushroom, cheese and lettuce or arugula; serve immediately. Serves 4.

Quick tip

Serve up a healthy veggie plate for dinner...a good old southern tradition. With 2 or 3 scrumptious veggie dishes and a basket of buttery cornbread, no one will miss the meat!

Irene's Portabella Burgers

Spicy Black Bean Scrambled Eggs

Donna Jones, Mikado, MI

One day, I had lots of my mother-in-law's homemade salsa on hand and some leftover black beans in the fridge. Added to typically boring scrambled eggs, the result was a dish I couldn't get enough of. Try it, you'll like it too!

1/4 c. canned black beans, drained and rinsed
1/4 c. chunky salsa
1/8 t. chili powder
Optional: 1/8 t. red pepper flakes
2 eggs, beaten
6-inch corn tortilla
1/4 c. shredded sharp Cheddar cheese
Optional: additional salsa

Spray a small skillet with non-stick vegetable spray. Over medium heat, cook beans, salsa and desired seasonings for one minute, stirring frequently. Add eggs; stir to combine. Continue cooking and stirring until eggs are fully cooked. Place tortilla on a microwave-safe dinner plate and microwave for 10 seconds, until warmed. Spoon egg mixture onto tortilla. Top with cheese and more salsa, if desired. Serve immediately. Makes one serving.

Herbed Mushroom Omelets

Jo Ann

4 to 6 eggs, beaten
1 T. fresh parsley, chopped
1 t. fresh oregano, chopped
1/2 t. fresh thyme, chopped
salt and pepper to taste
2 t. butter, divided
1-1/2 c. sliced mushrooms

Whisk together eggs and seasonings; set aside. Melt one teaspoon butter in a skillet over medium heat. Add mushrooms and sauté until tender; remove from skillet and set aside. Melt 1/2 teaspoon butter in skillet over low heat; pour in half the egg mixture. Stir eggs around in skillet with a spatula to cook evenly. Lift edges to allow uncooked egg to flow underneath. When almost cooked, spoon on half the mushrooms and fold over. Repeat with remaining egg mixture. Serves 2.

Use any favorites from your herb garden...rosemary and chives are really good too. The sautéed mushrooms give a golden brown look to this pretty omelet. —Jo Ann

Herbed Mushroom Omelets

Suzanne's Tomato Melt

Suzanne's Tomato Melt

Audrey Lett, Newark, DE

I love this as a quick dinner with a fresh salad...it is so easy to make!

1/4 c. shredded Cheddar cheese
1 onion bagel or English muffin, split
2 tomato slices
1 T. Parmesan cheese
fresh basil leaves

Sprinkle half the Cheddar cheese over each bagel or English muffin half. Top with a tomato slice. Sprinkle half the Parmesan cheese over each tomato. Add fresh basil leaf on top. Broil about 6 inches from heat for 4 to 5 minutes, or until cheese is bubbly. Makes one serving.

Simple Scalloped Tomatoes

Joan White, Malvern, PA

This tangy-sweet dish makes a delicious dinner. Serve with cheese bread for a complete meal.

1 onion, chopped
1/4 c. butter
28-oz. can diced tomatoes
5 slices bread, lightly toasted and cubed
1/4 c. brown sugar, packed
1/2 t. salt
1/4 t. pepper

Cook onion in butter until just tender, but not browned. Combine onion mixture with tomatoes and their juice in a bowl; add remaining ingredients, and mix well. Pour into a greased 8"x8" baking pan. Bake, uncovered, at 350 degrees for 45 minutes. Serves 4 to 6.

Quick tip

No more trying to keep tomato plants upright in the garden. Plant pint-size cherry tomato plants in hanging baskets filled with potting soil. They'll grow beautifully...upside-down!

Simple Scalloped Tomatoes

Baked Garden Omelet

Gwen Hudson, Madison Heights, VA

I serve this scrumptious vegetable-packed dish year 'round for a light dinner. Feel free to add your favorite fresh veggies!

2-1/2 c. shredded cheeses, Pepper Jack, Cheddar, Colby or combination of cheeses, divided
1-1/2 c. broccoli, chopped
2 tomatoes, coarsely chopped
1 c. milk
1/4 c. all-purpose flour
1/2 t. salt
3 eggs, beaten

In an ungreased 8"x8" baking pan, layer half of the cheese, broccoli, tomatoes and remaining cheese; set aside. In a bowl, beat milk, flour, salt and eggs until smooth. Pour over cheese mixture. Bake, uncovered, at 350 degrees for 40 to 45 minutes, until set. Let stand 10 minutes before cutting into squares. Serves 6 to 8.

I really like stir-fry and chow mein, so I created this recipe using the items that I had in my garden and fridge. It is now one of my family's favorites and makes great leftovers too. —Melinda

Melinda's Veggie Stir-Fry

Melinda Daniels, Lewiston, ID

8-oz. pkg. spaghetti, uncooked
2 c. broccoli, cut into bite-size flowerets
1 c. snow or sugar snap pea pods, halved
2 carrots, peeled and thinly sliced
1/2 onion, thinly sliced
1/4 green pepper, thinly sliced

Cook spaghetti as package directs; drain and set aside. Meanwhile, place vegetables into a steamer basket; place in a large stockpot filled with enough water to just reach the bottom of the basket. Heat over medium heat and steam for about 3 to 5 minutes, until just beginning to soften; drain. If crisper vegetables are desired, omit this step. When spaghetti and vegetables are done, add to Stir-Fry Sauce in skillet. Cook and stir over medium-high heat for about 15 minutes, to desired tenderness. Serves 6 to 8.

Stir-Fry Sauce:

1/2 c. olive oil
1/3 c. soy sauce
2 T. Dijon mustard
2 T. sliced pepperoncini, chopped
2 cloves garlic, minced
1 t. pepper

In a large skillet over low heat, mix all ingredients together. Simmer until heated through.

Melinda's Veggie Stir-Fry

Trail Mix Bagels

Becky Drees, Pittsfield, MA

Perfect for an on-the-go dinner, lunch or hike...a tasty energy boost!

8-oz. pkg. cream cheese, softened
1 T. lemon juice
1/2 c. raisins
1 carrot, peeled and grated
1/3 c. trail mix, coarsely chopped, or sunflower kernels
4 bagels, split

Place cream cheese in a bowl. Add remaining ingredients except bagels; stir until well blended and creamy. Spread between sliced bagels. Makes 4 servings.

Trail Mix Bagels

Strawberry Patch Sandwich

Shelley Turner, Boise, ID

Try the banana bread...it's oh-so-yummy paired with peanut butter and fresh strawberries.

2 slices whole-wheat bread or banana bread
1 T. creamy peanut butter
1 T. cream cheese, softened
2 strawberries, hulled and sliced
1 t. honey

Spread one slice of bread with peanut butter. Spread remaining slice with cream cheese. Arrange strawberry slices in a single layer over peanut butter. Drizzle honey over berries; close sandwich. Makes one sandwich.

Scott's Wonderful Waffles

Sheila Murray, Tehachapi, CA

My son came up with this recipe and made it for the whole family. It was a great hit!

1 c. milk
1/2 c. oil
3 eggs, beaten
1-1/2 c. cherry pie filling
18-1/2 oz. pkg. yellow cake mix
Garnish: butter, maple syrup

In a bowl, mix all ingredients except garnish. Refrigerate until waffle iron is ready. Ladle batter by 1/2 cupfuls onto a lightly greased preheated waffle iron; bake according to manufacturer's directions. Garnish as desired. Makes 8 to 10 waffles.

Texas Toads in the Hole

Uncle Dave's Oven Pancakes

Anne Ptacnik, Yuma, CO

My late Uncle Dave often made these yummy pancakes when I was a guest at his home. Now, whenever I prepare them, I think about him and how he always made everything so very special.

1/4 c. butter
4 eggs, beaten
2 c. milk
1 c. all-purpose flour
1/2 c. sugar
Garnish: butter, pancake syrup

Place butter in a 13"x9" baking pan; melt in a 400-degree oven. Add eggs, milk, flour and sugar to a bowl; whisk until thoroughly combined. Pour mixture over melted butter. Bake at 350 degrees for 30 minutes. Cut and serve with butter and syrup. Serves 4 to 6.

Texas Toads in the Hole

Elizabeth Holcomb, Canyon Lake, TX

2 T. butter
4 slices Texas toast
4 eggs
salt and pepper to taste
Optional: jam, jelly or preserves

Spread butter on both sides of Texas toast. Using a biscuit cutter, cut a circle out of the middle of each slice of toast; set aside rounds. Place toast slices in a large, lightly greased skillet over medium heat; break an egg into each hole. Season with salt and pepper. Cook until egg white begins to set, then carefully flip. Continue to cook until eggs reach desired doneness. In a separate skillet, toast reserved bread rounds. Top rounds with jam, jelly or preserves, if desired. Serve with toast slices. Serves 4.

I made this recipe for my girls when they were little. They always loved it because of the funny name, as well as the fact they had eggs and toast all in one dish! —Elizabeth

Creamy Italian Noodles

Beth Shaeffer, Greenwood, IN

These zesty noodles are so quick and easy to prepare...a super alternative to rice or potatoes.

8-oz. pkg. thin egg noodles, uncooked
1/4 c. butter, sliced
1/2 c. evaporated milk or half-and-half
1/4 c. grated Parmesan cheese
2-1/4 t. Italian salad dressing mix

In a saucepan, cook egg noodles according to package directions; drain and set aside. In the same saucepan, melt butter. Return noodles to pan; add milk or half-and-half and cheese. Stir to combine; add dressing mix and stir again. Serves 4.

Eggs Benedict

Diana Chaney, Olathe, KS

Who knew a dish that looks this elegant would be so easy? Nothing beats these eggs paired with a fresh green salad for dinner.

8 slices Canadian bacon
1 t. lemon juice or vinegar
8 eggs
4 English muffins, split and toasted
3 T. butter, softened and divided
1 c. Hollandaise sauce, divided
Garnish: chopped fresh chives

Brown bacon in a skillet over medium heat. Meanwhile, fill a large saucepan with 2 inches of water and lemon juice or vinegar; bring to a simmer. Crack each egg into a shallow bowl and slip them, one at a time, into the water. Poach for about 3 minutes, until whites are set and yolks are soft. Remove eggs with a slotted spoon and drain on paper towels. Top each toasted muffin half with one teaspoon butter, one slice of bacon, one egg and a drizzle of Hollandaise sauce. Garnish with chives. Serves 4.

Grandma McKindley's Waffles

Nicole Millard, Mendon, MI

You can't go wrong with an old-fashioned waffle dinner...the topping choices are endless!

2 c. all-purpose flour
1 T. baking powder
1/4 t. salt
2 eggs, separated
1-1/2 c. milk
3 T. butter, melted
Garnish: fresh berries, maple syrup

Sift together flour, baking powder and salt; set aside. With an electric mixer on high speed, beat egg whites until stiff; set aside. Stir egg yolks, milk and melted butter together and add to dry ingredients, stirring just until moistened. Fold in egg whites. Ladle batter by 1/2 cupfuls onto a lightly greased preheated waffle iron; bake according to manufacturer's directions. Garnish as desired. Makes 8 to 10 waffles.

Grandma McKindley's Waffles

Mom's Macaroni & Cheese

Mom's Macaroni & Cheese

Billie Schettino, Kansas City, KS

1 c. elbow macaroni, uncooked
salt and pepper to taste
2 c. shredded American-Cheddar Jack cheese blend,
  divided
1 egg
1/2 c. skim milk
1/2 c. cottage cheese
2 to 3 T. butter, diced

Cook macaroni according to package directions; drain. Place half of macaroni into a 2-quart casserole dish coated with butter-flavored non-stick vegetable spray. Sprinkle macaroni with salt, pepper and one cup shredded cheese. Repeat layering. In a food processor, process egg, milk and cottage cheese until smooth. Pour mixture over top; dot with butter. Bake, uncovered, at 350 degrees for 30 to 45 minutes, until heated through and set. Cool slightly before serving. Serves 2 to 4.

Mom made this recipe for meatless Fridays. I always looked forward to it, even though I didn't like the spinach she served with it. Before I could eat my mac & cheese I had to eat at least one spoonful of spinach, which I did, and quickly washed it down with a big gulp of milk. It was worth it! —Billie

Tasty Tortilla Stack Pie

Connie Lufriu, Brandon, FL

My children ask for this often! I made it up one night when I was running low on groceries. Now it is a favorite dinner that they ask for at least once a week! It bakes up like a casserole but cuts up into little individual servings. What could be easier?

10-3/4 oz. can Cheddar cheese soup
1 t. chili powder
1 t. taco seasoning mix
4 6-inch flour tortillas
1/2 c. shredded Cheddar cheese
Garnish: sour cream, salsa

Stir together soup and seasonings. Place one tortilla in the bottom of an ungreased 9" round springform pan. Spoon 1/3 of mixture on top and sprinkle with a little cheese. Repeat layers, ending with cheese on top. Cover with aluminum foil. Bake at 350 degrees for about 20 minutes, until heated through and cheese is melted. To serve, cut into wedges; garnish as desired. Serves 4 to 5.

Broccoli Quiche Peppers

Broccoli Quiche Peppers

Cheri Maxwell, Gulf Breeze, FL

We love these colorful peppers for a dinner that's just a little different.

4 red, yellow or green peppers, tops cut off and reserved
4 eggs
1/2 c. milk
1 c. broccoli, finely chopped
1/2 t. garlic powder
1/4 t. Italian seasoning
Optional: shredded mozzarella cheese

Finely dice reserved tops of peppers; set aside. Place pepper shells upright in custard cups; set cups in a 9"x9" baking pan. In a bowl, whisk together eggs, milk, broccoli, diced pepper and seasonings; pour evenly into peppers. Bake, uncovered, at 325 degrees for 40 to 50 minutes, until peppers are tender and egg mixture is set. Top with cheese if desired and bake 10 more minutes. Let stand 5 minutes before serving. Makes 4 servings.

Angie's Pasta & Sauce

Angie Whitmore, Farmington, UT

6 to 8 roma tomatoes, halved, seeded and diced
1 to 2 cloves garlic, minced
1/2 c. butter, melted
1 T. dried basil
8-oz. pkg. angel hair pasta, cooked
Garnish: freshly grated Parmesan cheese

Combine tomatoes and garlic in a saucepan. Simmer over medium heat 15 minutes; set aside. Blend together butter and basil; add to pasta. Toss to coat. Stir in tomato mixture and garnish. Serves 4 to 6.

Homemade sauce is so simple to prepare. You'll love the taste of both the sauce and the freshly grated Parmesan on top. —Angie

Angie's Pasta & Sauce

Poppy's Onion Pizza

Lisa Arning, Garden City, NY

For a light vegetarian dinner, this pizza is the best choice.

3 T. olive oil, divided
10-inch refrigerated pizza crust
2 onions, diced
garlic powder to taste
paprika to taste
Optional: salt and pepper to taste

Lightly coat pizza pan with one tablespoon olive oil; place pizza dough into pan. Coat dough with one tablespoon olive oil; set aside. Sauté onions in remaining olive oil until golden; spread evenly over the pizza dough, lightly pressing down. Sprinkle with garlic powder and paprika; add salt and pepper, if desired. Bake at 425 degrees for 20 minutes or until golden. Serves 8.

Poppy's Onion Pizza

Creamy Fettuccine Alfredo

Sheila Bane, Waynetown, IN

This has been one of my tried & true recipes for over twenty years. It's a favorite of my kids...try it and you'll agree!

16-oz. pkg. fettuccine pasta, uncooked
1 t. salt
2/3 c. butter, softened
1-1/2 c. half-and-half, room temperature, divided
1-1/2 c. shredded Parmesan cheese
1/4 t. garlic salt
Garnish: additional shredded Parmesan cheese

Cook pasta as package directs, adding salt to cooking water. Remove pan from heat; drain pasta and return to pan. Add butter to warm pasta and mix well. Add 3/4 cup half-and-half to pasta; mix well. In a small bowl, mix together cheese and garlic salt. Add half of cheese mixture. Add remaining half-and-half and remaining cheese mixture to pasta mixture, stirring well after each addition. Garnish with additional cheese and serve immediately. Makes 6 servings.

Quick tip

For a no-fuss, low-fat, meatless meal, spoon grilled veggies onto a softened tortilla and roll up...delicious!

Creamy Fettuccine Alfredo

Dad's Famous French Toast

Annette Mullan, North Arlington, NJ

When I was growing up, my dad fixed French toast every Sunday morning from his own recipe. Sometimes he made it for a special dinner, too! Dad is no longer with us, but recently our family got together for a weekend and we made his French toast for everyone! It's still the best I've ever had.

4 eggs, beaten
1/2 c. milk
1/3 c. sugar
1 t. vanilla extract
1/8 t. cinnamon
1 loaf sliced white bread
Garnish: butter, pancake syrup, powdered sugar

Mix eggs, milk, sugar, vanilla and cinnamon in a large bowl. Dip bread into mixture, one slice at a time. Spray an electric or regular griddle with non-stick vegetable spray. Add bread slices; cook over medium heat until golden on both sides. Serve with desired garnishes. Serves 8.

Spinach & Tomato French Toast

Linda Bonwill. Englewood, FL

A healthier way to make French toast...plus, it looks so pretty!

3 eggs
salt and pepper to taste
8 slices Italian bread
4 c. fresh spinach, torn
2 tomatoes, sliced
Garnish: grated Parmesan cheese

In a bowl, beat eggs with salt and pepper. Dip bread slices into egg. Place in a lightly greased skillet over medium heat; cook one side until lightly golden. Place fresh spinach and 2 slices of tomato onto each slice, pressing lightly to secure. Flip and briefly cook on other side until golden. Serves 4.

Peanut Butter French Toast

Julie Perkins, Anderson, IN

Who can resist the classic taste of peanut butter & jelly?

4 slices white bread
1/2 c. creamy peanut butter
2 T. grape jelly
3 eggs, beaten
1/4 c. milk
2 T. butter
Garnish: powdered sugar

Use bread, peanut butter and jelly to make 2 sandwiches; set aside. In a bowl, whisk together eggs and milk. Dip each sandwich into egg mixture. Melt butter in a non-stick skillet over medium heat. Add sandwiches to skillet and cook until golden, about 2 to 3 minutes on each side. Sprinkle with powdered sugar; cut diagonally into triangles. Serves 2.

Peanut Butter French Toast

Fried Pecan Okra

Fried Pecan Okra

You can use a 16-ounce package of frozen cut okra, thawed, if you'd rather have bite-size pieces.

1 c. pecans
1-1/2 c. biscuit baking mix
1 t. salt
1/2 t. pepper
2 10-oz. pkgs. frozen whole okra, thawed
peanut oil for frying

Place pecans in an even layer in a shallow pan. Bake at 350 degrees for 10 minutes or until lightly toasted, stirring occasionally. Process pecans, baking mix, and salt and pepper in a food processor until nuts are finely ground. Place pecan mixture in a large bowl. Add okra, tossing to coat. Gently press pecan mixture into okra. Pour oil to a depth of 2 inches into a Dutch oven or cast-iron skillet; heat to 350 degrees. Fry okra, in batches, turning once, for 5 to 6 minutes, until golden; drain on paper towels. Serves 6 to 8.

Vidalia Onion Side Dish

Quick tip

Try grilling onions wrapped in heavy-duty aluminum foil for about 12 to 15 minutes. Be sure to use only Vidalia or Texas Sweet onions. Yum!

Vidalia Onion Side Dish

Onion-lovers will rave over this tasty side item cooked in the microwave in minutes.

2 Vidalia onions
2 cubes beef bouillon
1 T. butter
Optional: fresh parsley, pepper

Peel onions; cut a thin slice from bottom and top of each one. Scoop out a one-inch-deep hole from the top of each onion. Place onions, top sides up, in a 2-quart microwave-safe dish with a lid. Add one bouillon cube and 1/2 tablespoon butter to shallow hole in each onion. Microwave, covered, on high for 8 to 10 minutes or until onion is tender. Garnish with fresh parsley and pepper, if desired. Serves 2.

Satisfying Salad Suppers

(served with tasty breads & crackers)

Toss together a healthy dinner in no time with salads that become the star of the meal. Mix up a beautiful Summer Spinach Salad using fresh greens or stir up a Marinated Broccoli Salad and serve with Kathy's Bacon Popovers. Shrimp & Orzo Salad is sure to become an asked-for dinner when you serve it with Delicious Quick Rolls. So count down to dinner with these fresh and filling salads made with 6 ingredients or less.

Soft Sesame Bread Sticks

Green Goddess Bacon Salad

Julie Ann Perkins, Anderson, IN

7 eggs, hard-boiled, peeled and sliced
7 to 12 slices bacon, chopped and crisply cooked
3 c. deli roast chicken, shredded
6 to 8 c. baby spinach
1 red pepper, chopped
Optional: 1 bunch green onions, sliced
Green Goddess salad dressing to taste

In a large salad bowl, combine eggs, bacon, chicken and vegetables; mix well. Pass salad dressing at the table so guests may add it to taste. Makes 6 servings.

Soft Sesame Bread Sticks

Lynn Williams, Muncie, IN

Delicious with just about any dinner!

1-1/4 c. all-purpose flour
2 t. sugar
1-1/2 t. baking powder
1/2 t. salt
2/3 c. milk
2 T. butter, melted
2 t. sesame seed

In a small bowl, combine flour, sugar, baking powder and salt. Gradually add milk; stir to form a soft dough. Turn onto a floured surface; knead gently 3 to 4 times. Roll into a 10-inch by 5-1/2 inch rectangle; cut into 12 bread sticks. Place butter in a 13"x9" baking pan; coat bread sticks in butter and sprinkle with sesame seed. Bake at 450 degrees for 14 to 18 minutes, until golden. Makes one dozen.

I grew up loving Green Goddess dressing, my grandmother used it all the time. We relished salads, especially when everything was fresh from the garden or readily available at the Main Street fruit market! The family-owned market is still there...how blessed we are. —Julie

Green Goddess Bacon Salad

Mama's Cucumber Salad

Mama's Cucumber Salad

Virginia Shaw, Medon, TN

I used to take this salad to my sons' baseball award dinners and picnics. Children and adults alike always request this salad...it's cool, refreshing and very simple to make.

2 cucumbers, sliced
1 bunch green onions, diced, or 1 red onion, sliced
  and separated into rings
2 to 3 tomatoes, diced
1/2 c. zesty Italian salad dressing

Toss together vegetables in a large bowl; pour salad dressing over all and toss to mix. Cover and refrigerate at least 3 hours to overnight. Makes 8 to 10 servings.

Kelly's Easy Caramel Rolls

Kelly Marshall, Olathe, KS

This is a much-requested family recipe! Serve with a tossed salad for a special dinner.

3 T. corn syrup, divided
3 T. brown sugar, packed and divided
3 T. chopped pecans, divided
2 T. butter, cubed and divided
12-oz. tube refrigerated biscuits

To each of 10 greased muffin cups, add one teaspoon each of syrup, brown sugar and pecans. Top each with 1/2 teaspoon butter and one biscuit. Bake at 400 degrees for 8 to 10 minutes, until golden. Invert rolls onto a plate before serving. Makes 10 rolls.

Kelly's Easy Caramel Rolls

Delicious Quick Rolls

Ursula Juarez-Wall, Dumfries, VA

1 c. water
1 env. active dry yeast
2 T. sugar
2 T. shortening, melted
1 egg, beaten
2-1/4 c. all-purpose flour
1 t. salt

Heat water until very warm, about 110 to 115 degrees. In a large bowl, dissolve yeast in warm water. Add remaining ingredients; beat until smooth. Cover and let rise until double in size, about 30 to 60 minutes. Punch down. Form dough into 12 balls and place in a greased muffin pan. Cover and let rise again until double, about 30 minutes. Bake at 350 degrees for 15 minutes, or until golden. Makes one dozen.

My Grandma Bohannon is the most amazing woman I know! Not a single holiday meal passed without Grandma's piping-hot rolls on the table, and for decades she made dozens & dozens of rolls to sell to her neighbors. At ninety-nine years of age, she no longer bakes, so I am glad to share this recipe of hers. —Ursula

Delicious Quick Rolls

Island Chicken Salad

Carol Hickman, Kingsport, TN

Pile high on a lettuce leaf or serve on fresh croissants for a quick sandwich.

10-oz. can chunk white chicken, drained
8-oz. can crushed pineapple, drained
2 stalks celery, diced
1/2 c. cream cheese, softened
2 T. mayonnaise
Garnish: sliced almonds

Mix all ingredients together until well blended; chill. Makes 4 servings.

Island Chicken Salad

Caprese Salad

Caprese Salad

Beth Flack, Terre Haute, IN

Very refreshing! This is one of my favorite summer salads. Try it with cherry tomatoes and mini mozzarella balls too.

2 beefsteak tomatoes, sliced
4-oz. pkg. fresh mozzarella cheese, sliced
8 leaves fresh basil
Italian salad dressing to taste

Layer tomatoes, cheese slices and basil leaves in rows or in a circle around a large platter. Sprinkle with salad dressing. Cover and chill for one hour before serving. Serves 6.

Ryan's Yummy Pasta Salad

Chris Taylor, Bountiful, UT

My picky ten-year-old's favorite salad!

8-oz. pkg. refrigerated cheese tortellini, uncooked
2-1/2 c. rotelle pasta, uncooked
1 c. frozen mixed vegetables
1 c. deli roast chicken, chopped
2 T. lemon pepper, or to taste
ranch salad dressing to taste

In separate saucepans, cook tortellini and rotelle according to package directions, adding frozen vegetables to pasta pan. Drain; combine in a large serving bowl. Add chicken to pasta; sprinkle generously with lemon pepper. Add salad dressing to desired consistency and toss to mix. May be served warm or chilled. Serves 6 to 8.

Chicken-Broccoli Rotini Salad

Debbie Cutelli, Saint Louis, MO

I've served this delicious salad often at ladies' luncheons and showers but it makes a great dinner salad as well!

2-1/2 c. rotini pasta, uncooked
2 c. cooked chicken, cubed
1/2 c. Italian salad dressing
2 c. broccoli, cut into bite-size flowerets
1/2 c. red pepper, chopped

Cook pasta according to package directions; drain and rinse with cold water. In a large bowl, mix pasta with chicken and Italian salad dressing. Cover and refrigerate for one hour. Add broccoli, red pepper and Parmesan Dressing; toss to mix. Cover and refrigerate until serving time. Makes about 6 servings.

Parmesan Dressing:

1 c. grated Parmesan cheese
1/2 c. olive oil
2 T. lemon juice
1/8 t. dried basil

In a bowl, whisk all ingredients together.

Fresh Kale Salad

Fresh Kale Salad

Carol Werner, Brooklyn Park, MN

This recipe goes together so quickly, and is very healthy and tasty to boot!

3 T. honey
1/2 c. olive or canola oil
juice of 1 lemon
pepper to taste
1 bunch fresh kale, torn and stems removed
1/2 c. raisins or dried cranberries
1/4 c. sunflower kernels

In a large bowl, combine honey, oil, lemon juice and pepper. Whisk until blended. Add kale and toss to coat; let stand about 5 minutes. Sprinkle with raisins or cranberries and sunflower seeds; toss again. Serves 6.

Chunky Tomato-Avocado Salad

Alma Evans, Patrick, FL

Let this flavorful salad sit for at least two hours if you don't have time to refrigerate it overnight. The flavors blend together so beautifully!

1 avocado, pitted, peeled and cubed
3 plum tomatoes, chopped
1/2 c. sweet onion, chopped
1 T. fresh cilantro, chopped
2 to 3 T. lemon juice

Gently stir together all ingredients; cover and refrigerate overnight. Serves 4.

Chunky Tomato-Avocado Salad

Crab & Broccoli Rolls

Jane Moore. Haverford, PA

Season with onion or garlic salt to taste or spice up with a dash of hot pepper sauce!

6-oz. can flaked crabmeat, drained

10-oz. pkg. frozen chopped broccoli, cooked, drained and cooled

1/4 c. mayonnaise

1/2 c. shredded Swiss cheese

8-oz. tube refrigerated crescent rolls, separated

Combine crab, broccoli, mayonnaise and cheese; spread about 2 tablespoonfuls on each crescent. Roll up crescent roll-style; arrange on a lightly greased baking sheet. Bake at 375 degrees for 20 minutes. Makes 8.

Cheddar-Dill Bread

Julie Ann Perkins, Anderson, IN

Total comfort after a busy day at work. Never miss a chance to enjoy a slice of warm bread with a fresh salad!

2 c. self-rising flour

1/4 c. butter

1 c. shredded Cheddar cheese

2 t. dill weed

1 egg

3/4 c. milk

Place flour in a large bowl. Cut in butter with 2 knives until crumbly; stir in cheese and dill. In a small bowl, beat egg and milk; add to flour mixture and stir just until moistened. Batter will be thick. Spoon into a greased 9"x5" loaf pan. Bake at 350 degrees for 35 to 40 minutes, until bread tests done with a toothpick inserted in the center. Cool loaf in pan 10 minutes; turn out of pan and serve warm. Makes one loaf.

Summer Spinach Salad

Judy Manning, Great Bend, KS

1 lb. spinach, torn

3 eggs, hard-boiled, peeled and sliced

8 slices bacon, crisply cooked and crumbled

6 green onions, thinly sliced

Arrange all ingredients in a salad bowl. Cover and refrigerate for about 2 hours. At serving time, shake Cider Vinegar Dressing and drizzle over salad. Toss until spinach is well coated; serve at once. Makes 6 servings.

Cider Vinegar Dressing:

1/4 c. olive oil

1/4 c. cider vinegar

1 t. salt

1/8 t. pepper

1 clove garlic, quartered

Combine all ingredients in a jar with a tight-fitting lid; shake vigorously. Refrigerate. At serving time, remove garlic and discard.

This salad is always made at our home with the first crop of fresh homegrown spinach and green onions. Serve with biscuits or cheese rolls for a quick weeknight dinner. —Judy

Summer Spinach Salad

Swope Bread

Dan Needham, Columbus, OH

My grandmother used to make this simple batter bread. We never did find out where the name came from, but it is tasty and easy to make. Serve with a favorite chicken salad.

2 c. whole-wheat flour
1 c. all-purpose flour
1/2 c. sugar
1 t. salt
2 t. baking soda
2 c. buttermilk
Optional: 3/4 c. raisins

In a large bowl, stir together flours, sugar and salt; set aside. In a separate bowl, dissolve baking soda in buttermilk. Stir buttermilk mixture into flour mixture; beat well. Fold in raisins, if desired. Pour batter into a lightly greased 9"x5" loaf pan. Bake at 350 degrees for one hour, until golden. Cool on a wire rack. Makes one loaf.

Lemon-Herb Chicken Salad

Barbara Burke, Gulfport, MS

The lemon-herb dressing makes this chicken salad just a little different. It's especially good with a rustic brown bread.

2 boneless, skinless chicken breasts, cooked and diced
1/4 c. mayonnaise
1/4 c. plain yogurt
1 T. fresh dill, chopped
2 t. lemon juice
1/2 t. lemon zest
1/4 t. salt

Place chicken in a serving bowl; set aside. Combine remaining ingredients; mix well and toss with chicken. Chill before serving. Serves 4 to 6.

Swope Bread

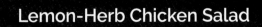

Lemon-Herb Chicken Salad

Sweet Ambrosia Salad

Rachel Ripley, Pittsburgh, PA

Kids of all ages love this sweet, creamy salad!

20-oz. can pineapple chunks, drained
14-1/2 oz. jar maraschino cherries, drained
11-oz. can mandarin oranges, drained
8-oz. container sour cream
10-1/2 oz. pkg. pastel mini marshmallows
1/2 c. sweetened flaked coconut

Combine fruit in a large bowl; stir in sour cream until coated. Fold in marshmallows and coconut; cover and chill overnight. Makes 8 to 10 servings.

Sweet Ambrosia Salad

Sesame-Asparagus Salad

Kathy Milliga, Mira, Loma, CA

Our family loves this salad in springtime when asparagus is fresh...it tastes terrific and is easy to prepare.

1-1/2 lbs. asparagus, cut diagonally into 2-inch pieces
3 T. toasted sesame oil
1 t. white wine vinegar
4 t. soy sauce
2-1/2 T. sugar or honey
4 t. toasted sesame seed

Bring a large saucepan of water to a boil over high heat. Add asparagus; cook for 2 to 3 minutes, just until crisp-tender. Immediately drain asparagus; rinse with cold water until asparagus is completely cooled. Drain again; pat dry. Cover and refrigerate until chilled, about one hour. In a small bowl, whisk together remaining ingredients; cover and refrigerate. At serving time, drizzle asparagus with dressing; toss to coat. Makes 4 to 6 servings.

Quick tip

Choose local, seasonal fresh fruits and vegetables instead of ones that have shipped a long distance. You'll be serving your family the freshest, tastiest produce year-round at the lowest prices.

Sesame-Asparagus Salad

Lucy's Sausage Salad

Lucy's Sausage Salad

Lucy Davis, Colorado Springs, CO

This deliciously different salad may be made ahead and chilled for one to two hours, or served immediately.

14-oz. pkg. mini smoked beef sausages, divided
1 t. canola oil
1 c. corn
15-1/2 oz. can black beans, drained and rinsed
1 T. canned jalapeño pepper, seeded and minced
1 c. red pepper, chopped
Garnish: fresh cilantro sprigs

Measure out half the sausages; set aside for a future use. Slice remaining sausages into 3 pieces each. In a skillet, sauté sausages in oil over medium heat until lightly golden; drain. In a large bowl, combine corn, beans, jalapeño and red pepper. Stir in sausage. Toss with Dressing; garnish with cilantro. Serves 4.

Dressing:
3 T. low-fat plain yogurt
3 T. low-fat sour cream
1/4 c. picante sauce
1/2 c. fresh cilantro, chopped
salt and pepper to taste

Whisk together all ingredients.

Bacon-y Romaine Salad

Meredith Schaller, Watertown, WI

The savory, sweet bacon dressing makes this salad unforgettable!

2 heads romaine lettuce, chopped
1 sweet onion, thinly sliced
1/2 lb. bacon, chopped
1 c. cider vinegar
1 c. sugar

Arrange lettuce in a large serving bowl. Layer onion on top. Cook bacon in a skillet over medium-high heat until crisp; drain. Combine vinegar and sugar; pour into skillet with bacon. Bring to a simmer over medium heat. Cook and stir vinegar mixture until sugar dissolves. Pour mixture over lettuce and onion. Toss together and serve immediately. Serves 8.

Shrimp & Orzo Salad

Rosemary LightBown, Wakefield, RI

Everyone loves this yummy salad...and it's so easy to make!

1-1/2 c. orzo pasta, uncooked
1 c. asparagus, trimmed
1 c. cooked medium shrimp
3 green onions, thinly sliced
1/2 c. fresh parsley, chopped
Italian salad dressing to taste

Cook orzo according to package directions; drain. Place asparagus in a large saucepan of simmering water for 3 to 4x minutes. Rinse with cold water; slice into bite-size pieces. Mix orzo, asparagus, shrimp, onions, and parsley. Drizzle with salad dressing; toss to mix. Serves 6.

Crabby Tuna Salad

Joan Dove, Millersville, MD

You'll be happy, not crabby, when you taste this salad!

2 c. cooked elbow macaroni
6-oz. can tuna, drained
1/4 to 1/2 c. mayonnaise
2 T. onion, chopped
2 T. celery, chopped
2 T. seafood seasoning

Rinse macaroni with cold water; drain well. Mix macaroni and tuna with enough mayonnaise to moisten; add onion, celery and seasoning. Mix well and chill. Serves 3 to 4.

Shrimp & Orzo Salad

Chilled Apple & Cheese Salad

Melody Taynor, Everett, WA

As a girl, I was convinced that I didn't like gelatin salads. But when my Aunt Clara served this at an anniversary party, I found I had been mistaken!

3-oz. pkg. lemon gelatin mix
1 c. boiling water
3/4 c. cold water
2/3 c. red apple, cored and finely chopped
1/3 c. shredded Cheddar cheese
1/4 c. celery, chopped

In a bowl, dissolve gelatin in boiling water. Stir in cold water; chill until partially set. Fold in remaining ingredients. Pour into a 3-cup mold. Cover and chill 3 hours, or until firm. Unmold onto a serving plate. Makes 6 servings.

Chilled Apple & Cheese Salad

Pea Salad

Dee Faulding, Santa Barbara, CA

This is a great salad to bring to any summer gathering or a sunny picnic in the park!

1 c. elbow macaroni, cooked
3 slices bacon, crisply cooked and crumbled
1/2 c. green onion, chopped
2 c. frozen baby peas, thawed
1 c. mayonnaise
1/2 c. shredded Cheddar cheese

In a bowl, combine macaroni, bacon, green onions and peas. Stir in mayonnaise; cover and refrigerate for at least 2 hours. Sprinkle with cheese just before serving. Serves 4 to 6.

Cream Cheese Crescent Rolls

Kris Thompson, Ripley, NY

My mother received this recipe from my cousin many years ago. It's quick & easy...no one can eat just one!

3-oz. pkg. cream cheese, softened
1/4 c. sugar
1 T. lemon juice
8-oz. tube refrigerated crescent rolls

In a small bowl, blend cream cheese, sugar and lemon juice until smooth. Separate rolls; spread each roll with cream cheese mixture. Roll up, starting at one long edge. Arrange rolls on a lightly greased baking sheet. Bake at 375 degrees for 12 to 15 minutes, until golden. Makes 8 rolls.

Apple-Walnut Chicken Salad

Becky Butler, Keller, TX

This tasty recipe uses the convenience of a roast chicken from your grocery store's deli...what a great time-saver!

6 c. mixed field greens or baby greens
2 c. deli roast chicken, shredded
1/3 c. crumbled blue cheese
1/4 c. chopped walnuts, toasted
1 Fuji or Gala apple, cored and chopped

In a large salad bowl, toss together all ingredients. Drizzle Balsamic Apple Vinaigrette over salad, tossing gently to coat. Serve immediately. Makes 6 servings.

Balsamic Apple Vinaigrette:

2 T. frozen apple juice concentrate
1 T. cider vinegar
1 T. white balsamic vinegar
1 t. Dijon mustard
1/4 t. garlic powder
1/3 c. olive oil

Whisk together all ingredients in a small bowl.

Apple-Walnut Chicken Salad

Kathy's Bacon Popovers

Kathy's Bacon Popovers

Kathy Grashoff, Fort Wayne, IN

Mmm...bacon! Serve these tasty popovers with a salad for a dinner they'll love!

2 eggs
1 c. milk
1 T. oil
1 c. all-purpose flour
1/2 t. salt
3 slices bacon, crisply cooked and crumbled

Whisk together eggs, milk and oil. Beat in flour and salt just until smooth. Fill 12 greased and floured muffin cups 2/3 full. Sprinkle bacon evenly over batter. Bake at 400 degrees for 25 to 30 minutes, until puffed and golden. Serve warm. Makes one dozen.

Marinated Broccoli Salad

Beverly Brown, Bowie, MD

So easy. . .you can mix in the bag! Be sure to let the flavors blend overnight.

2 bunches broccoli flowerets, chopped
1 t. dill weed
1/4 c. oil
1/4 c. red wine vinegar
2 cloves garlic, minced
Optional: sweetened, dried cranberries, sliced almonds

Place ingredients in a one-gallon plastic zipping bag; close and shake well. Refrigerate overnight, shaking occasionally; serve chilled. Serves 6.

Marinated Broccoli Salad

Busy-Day Banana Bread

Laura Justice, Indianapolis, IN

Super easy and freezes well. Keep some on hand to serve with a favorite chicken salad. Just pull from the freezer the night before and it will be ready for your busy day!

3 ripe bananas, mashed
3 eggs, beaten
1/2 c. butter, melted and slightly cooled
1 T. vanilla extract
1/2 c. water
18-1/2 oz. pkg. yellow cake mix

In a large bowl, blend together bananas, eggs, butter, vanilla and water. Gradually add dry cake mix. Beat with an electric mixer on high speed for 4 minutes. Pour batter into 2 greased 9"x5" loaf pans. Bake at 350 degrees for 40 minutes. Increase temperature to 400 degrees and bake an additional 5 to 10 minutes, until tops are golden. Makes 2 loaves.

Heavenly Rice

Linda Robinson, Diamond, IL

3-oz. pkg. strawberry gelatin mix
1/2 c. powdered sugar
1/2 c. boiling water
2 c. crushed pineapple, drained
1 c. cooked long-cooking rice, cooled
1 pt. whipping cream

Place dry gelatin mix and powdered sugar in a large bowl; add boiling water and stir well. Add pineapple and rice; mix well. With an electric mixer on high setting, whip cream until stiff peaks form. Fold whipped cream into gelatin mixture. Spoon into a serving bowl; cover and refrigerate for 2 hours to overnight. Makes 10 servings.

Busy-Day Banana Bread

My family enjoyed this yummy dish at every holiday for many years. Recently we were invited to my cousin's house for dinner, so I made Heavenly Rice and took it in the same bowl that my grandmother and mom had served it in. It brought back so many memories of family and togetherness! —Linda

Heavenly Rice

Crispy Corn Fritters

Karen Puchnick, Butler, PA

So easy to make...delicious with a pasta salad!

1 c. biscuit baking mix
1/2 c. milk
1 egg
1 c. frozen corn, thawed
pepper to taste
2 T. oil
Optional: honey

In a bowl, stir together baking mix, milk and egg until just blended. Stir in corn; season with pepper. Let batter stand for 5 to 10 minutes. Heat oil in a skillet over medium heat. Drop batter into oil with a large spoon. Cook until golden; turn and cook one minute on the other side. Drain on paper towels. Serve drizzled with a little honey if desired. Makes 6 to 8 servings.

Penne & Goat Cheese Salad

Claudia Olsen, Chester, NJ

One of my husband's favorite pasta salads...it's just a little different from most. Try arugula for a slightly spicy taste or feta cheese if you prefer it to goat cheese.

12-oz. pkg. penne pasta, uncooked
1 T. garlic, minced
1/4 c. mayonnaise
4-oz. pkg. goat cheese, diced
1/2 c. sun-dried tomatoes packed in oil, drained and oil reserved
2 c. baby spinach, coarsely chopped

Cook pasta according to package directions; drain and rinse with cold water. In a large bowl, combine pasta with garlic, mayonnaise and goat cheese. Finely chop tomatoes and add along with spinach; mix gently. Stir in reserved oil from tomatoes, one tablespoon at a time, until ingredients are nicely coated. Serve at room temperature, or cover and chill. Makes 8 servings.

Crispy Corn Fritters

Penne & Goat Cheese Salad

Crisp Celery-Pear Salad

Crisp Celery-Pear Salad

Stephanie Mayer, Portsmouth, VA

A wonderful quick-to-make, cool-weather salad...makes a delicious dinner too.

4 stalks celery, halved lengthwise
2 T. cider vinegar
2 T. honey
1/4 t. salt
2 red pears, cored and diced
8-oz. pkg. white Cheddar cheese, diced
pepper to taste
1/2 c. chopped pecans, toasted

Place celery in a bowl of ice water for 15 minutes. Drain celery and pat dry; slice 1/2-inch thick. Whisk together vinegar, honey and salt in a serving bowl. Add pears; gently stir to coat. Add celery and remaining ingredients; stir to combine. Serve at room temperature. If desired, make up to 2 hours ahead, reserving pecans. Chill; stir in pecans at serving time. Makes 6 servings.

Dilly Cucumber Salad

Debra Home, Victoria, Australia

4 c. cucumbers, peeled and thinly sliced
3/4 c. sour cream
1 t. sugar
1/2 t. garlic salt
1/2 t. salt
1/2 t. white vinegar
1/4 t. dill weed

Place sliced cucumbers in a serving bowl. Mix next 6 ingredients in a separate bowl; add to cucumbers and toss to coat. Sprinkle dill weed over salad. Cover and refrigerate for at least one hour. Mix lightly before serving. Serves 6.

When I moved to Australia, I brought along my Gooseberry Patch books. I absolutely love your books. I've even introduced some of my Aussie friends to them! —Debra

Dilly Cucumber Salad

Mile-High Buttermilk Biscuits

Mile-High Buttermilk Biscuits

Staci Meyers, Montezuma, GA

The secret? Use a sharp biscuit cutter and don't twist it when cutting out your biscuits...you'll be amazed how high they rise!

2 c. all-purpose flour
1 T. baking powder
1 t. salt
1/2 c. shortening, chilled in freezer
2/3 to 3/4 c. buttermilk
1/4 c. butter, melted

Mix together flour, baking powder and salt. Cut in shortening until mixture has a crumbly texture. Stir in buttermilk until incorporated and dough leaves sides of bowl. Dough will be sticky. Knead dough 3 to 4 times on a lightly floured surface. Roll out to 1/2-inch thickness, about 2 to 4 passes with a rolling pin. Cut dough with a biscuit cutter, pressing straight down with cutter. Place biscuits on a parchment paper-lined baking sheet. Bake at 500 degrees for 8 to 10 minutes. Brush tops of warm biscuits with melted butter. Makes about one dozen.

Greek Orzo Salad

Leslie Stimel, Columbus, Ohio

This salad is my own creation...feel free to add or subtract any of these ingredients to suit your own taste!

1/3 c. roasted red peppers, diced
1/4 c. kalamata olives, sliced
1 tomato, diced
2 c. orzo pasta, cooked
1/2 c. crumbled feta cheese
balsamic vinegar to taste

Combine peppers, olives and tomato in a medium bowl; set aside. Rinse orzo with cold water; drain well. Add orzo and feta cheese to pepper mixture; mix well. Drizzle with vinegar; stir again. Serve warm or chilled. Serves 4.

Greek Orzo Salad

Tuna Seashell Salad

Tuna Seashell Salad

Susan Brees, Lincoln, NE

16-oz. pkg. shell macaroni, cooked
12-oz. can tuna, drained
3 eggs, hard-boiled, peeled and diced
4-oz. pkg. mild Cheddar cheese, diced
1/2 to 1 c. mayonnaise-type salad dressing
1/4 c. sweet pickle relish

Rinse macaroni with cold water; drain well. Combine all ingredients in a large serving bowl; chill. Serves 6 to 8.

I took this yummy salad to a potluck party and it won 1st place! —Susan

Blue Cheese Cut-Out Crackers

Dress up any salad when you serve these rich blue cheese crackers. Make them in any shape you like or cut them into little squares and skip the cookie cutters!

1 c. all-purpose flour
7 T. butter, softened
7 T. crumbled blue cheese
1/2 t. dried parsley
1 egg yolk
4 t. whipping cream
salt and cayenne pepper to taste

Mix all ingredients together; let rest for 30 minutes. Roll dough out to about 1/8-inch thick. Use small cookie cutters to cut out crackers. Bake on ungreased baking sheets at 400 degrees for 8 to 10 minutes, just until golden. Let cool; remove carefully. Store in an airtight container. Makes 1-1/2 to 2 dozen.

Blue Cheese Cut-Out Crackers

Bowtie Salad
with Tomatoes & Zucchini

Ann Mathis, Biscoe, AR

I love to serve this salad in the summer after we've been to the farmers' market. We have to buy extra grape tomatoes because we snack on them on the way home! Add some grilled shrimp, chicken or beef flank steak if you want a heartier salad.

12-oz. pkg. bowtie pasta, uncooked
2 T. olive oil, or more to taste
juice of 1 lemon, or more to taste
salt and pepper to taste
2 zucchini, diced
1-1/4 c. grape tomatoes, halved
6-oz. container crumbled feta cheese
Garnish: 1/4 c. fresh parsley, minced

Cook pasta according to package directions; drain and rinse with cold water. Transfer pasta to a serving bowl. Add oil, lemon juice, salt and pepper; toss to mix. Add zucchini, tomatoes, and cheese; toss again. Add more oil or lemon juice, if desired. For best flavor, cover and refrigerate at least 2 hours. Garnish with fresh parsley just before serving. Serves 6.

Quick tip

Don't hesitate to stock up on frozen vegetables. Flash-frozen soon after being harvested, frozen veggies retain more nutrients than canned vegetables.

Confetti Corn & Rice Salad

Lois Carswell, Kennesaw, GA

This colorful salad is a favorite at our family gatherings and barbecues, especially during the summer when we can use fresh-picked sweet corn...yum!

4 ears corn, husked
1-1/2 c. cooked rice
1 red onion, thinly sliced
1 green pepper, halved and thinly sliced
1 pt. cherry tomatoes, halved
Optional: 1 jalapeño pepper, thinly sliced

Boil or grill ears of corn until tender; let cool. With a sharp knife, cut corn from cob in "planks." In a serving bowl, combine rice, red onion, green pepper, tomatoes and jalapeño pepper, if using. Mix in corn, keeping some corn planks for top. Drizzle with Simple Dressing. Serve at room temperature or refrigerate overnight before serving. Serves 8.

Simple Dressing:

2 T. red wine vinegar
2 T. olive oil
salt and pepper to taste

Whisk all ingredients together.

Confetti Corn & Rice Salad

Pop-in-the-Oven Casseroles & Quiches

(all-in-one meals they'll love)

With just a few ingredients and these tasty recipes, you can have a one-dish meal that you can make in no time! Try baking an Egg Casserole Deluxe loaded with cheese and bacon! Meatball-Stuffed Shells are super easy to make because you use purchased meatballs. Mexicali Chicken Stack-Ups are baked in the oven and then cut into yummy wedges of goodness for everyone to enjoy. So gather up those casserole pans and bake dinner tonight!

One-Pan Roast Chicken Dinner

Kathy Harris, Council Grove, KS

This is my go-to recipe whenever I need a fast, easy, nutritious dinner. The oven does all the work...I love how crisp the chicken gets and it's not even fried! Trust me, it goes together in no time.

6 T. olive oil, divided
2 lemons, divided
4 cloves garlic, minced
1 t. kosher salt
1/2 t. pepper
3/4 lb. fresh green beans, trimmed
8 new redskin potatoes, quartered
4 chicken thighs or breasts

Coat a 13"x9" baking pan or cast-iron skillet with one tablespoon olive oil. Thinly slice one lemon; arrange lemon slices in pan in a single layer and set aside. Squeeze juice from remaining lemon. In a large bowl, combine remaining oil, lemon juice, garlic, salt and pepper; add green beans and toss to coat. With a slotted spoon, arrange beans on top of lemon slices. Add potatoes to oil mixture; toss to coat. With slotted spoon, arrange potatoes around edge of pan, on top of beans. Add chicken to oil mixture and coat thoroughly. Place chicken in pan, skin-side up. Drizzle any remaining oil mixture over chicken. Bake, uncovered, at 450 degrees for 50 minutes, or until chicken juices run clear. Remove chicken to a plate; keep warm. Return beans and potatoes to oven for another 10 minutes, or until potatoes are fork tender. Serve each chicken piece with some of the beans and potatoes. Makes 4 servings.

Hunter's Pie

Heidi Maurer, Garrett, IN

My 3-year-old son Hunter loves this and my 8-year-old son Luke does too...but without the beans!

1 lb. roast beef, cooked and cubed
12-oz. jar beef gravy
1 16-oz. bag classic mixed vegetables (corn, carrots, peas, cut green beans) thawed
9-inch deep-dish pie crust, baked
11-oz. tube refrigerated bread sticks

Combine all ingredients except pie crust and bread sticks; spread into pie crust. Arrange unbaked bread sticks on top, criss-cross style. Bake at 350 degrees for 20 minutes, or until heated through and bread sticks are golden. Serves 4.

Cowboy Macaroni & Cheese

Linda McWilliams, Fillmore, NY

When my children were little I found they would try new recipes if I gave them special names. This name did the trick!

3 c. elbow macaroni, uncooked
10-3/4 oz. can cream of mushroom soup
1/2 c. milk
1/2 t. dry mustard
pepper to taste
Optional: hot dogs, cut into bite-size pieces
3 c. shredded Cheddar cheese, divided
2 c. French fried onions, divided

Cook macaroni according to package directions; drain and set aside. Blend soup, milk, mustard and pepper; stir in cooked macaroni, hot dogs if using and 2 cups cheese. Sprinkle with half the onions and mix well. Transfer to a 13"x9" baking pan sprayed with non-stick vegetable spray. Cover; bake at 400 degrees for 30 minutes. Remove from oven; top with remaining cheese and onions. Serves 6 to 8.

Hunter's Pie

Hashbrown Quiche

Sonya Labbe, Santa Monica, CA

The secret? The crust is made with frozen hashbrowns!

3 c. frozen shredded hashbrowns, thawed
1/4 c. butter, melted
3 eggs, beaten
1 c. half-and-half
1/2 c. green onions, chopped
1 c. shredded Cheddar cheese
salt and pepper to taste
Optional: 1 c. cooked ham, cubed

In an ungreased 9" pie plate, combine hashbrowns and butter. Press hashbrowns into the bottom and up the sides of the pie plate. Bake at 450 degrees for 20 to 25 minutes, until golden and crisp. Remove from oven and cool slightly. Meanwhile, combine remaining ingredients in a bowl. Pour mixture over hashbrowns. Lower oven temperature to 350 degrees; bake for 30 minutes, or until quiche is golden and set. Serves 4 to 6.

Hashbrown Quiche

Corned Beef Casserole

Sherri Starman, Des Moines, IA

Very quick to put together...and gone in a flash!

7-1/4 oz. pkg. macaroni & cheese
12-oz. can corned beef, chopped
10-3/4 oz. can cream of celery soup
10-3/4 oz. can cream of chicken soup
1/4 to 1/2 c. milk

Cook macaroni until tender; drain. Stir in beef and soups; mix well. Add half the cheese packet from the box of macaroni & cheese; stir in milk. Pour into an ungreased 2-quart casserole dish; sprinkle remaining cheese on top. Bake at 350 degrees for one hour. Serves 4.

Parmesan Scalloped Potatoes

Tina Goodpasture, Meadowview, VA

Whether you eat them hot, cold or warm...these are some great scalloped potatoes!

2 lbs. Yukon Gold potatoes, thinly sliced
3 c. whipping cream
1/4 c. fresh parsley, chopped
2 cloves garlic, chopped
1-1/2 t. salt
1/4 t. pepper
1/3 c. grated Parmesan cheese

Layer potatoes in a lightly greased 3-quart casserole dish. In a bowl, stir together remaining ingredients except cheese; pour over potatoes. Bake, uncovered, at 400 degrees for 30 minutes, stirring gently every 10 minutes. Sprinkle with cheese; bake again for about 15 minutes, or until bubbly and golden. Let stand 10 minutes before serving. Serves 8.

Parmesan Scalloped Potatoes

My Mom's Stuffed Peppers

Nancy Girard, Chesapeake, VA

Mom made this quite often while I was growing up...it's now one of my children's favorites too!

3 green peppers, halved and seeded
1 lb. lean ground beef
10-3/4 oz. can tomato soup
1/4 c. long-cooking rice, uncooked
1 T. dried, minced onion
8-oz. can tomato sauce

Arrange pepper halves in an ungreased 13"x9" baking pan. In a bowl, mix together remaining ingredients except tomato sauce. Stuff peppers evenly with beef mixture. Spoon tomato sauce over peppers. Cover with aluminum foil. Bake at 350 degrees for one hour, or until peppers are tender and beef is cooked through. Serves 3 to 4.

Cheese & Onion Pie

Jane Kirsch, Weymouth, MA

Originally an English dish, this savory pie is absolutely delicious.

4 c. onions, thinly sliced
1 T. butter
2 c. favorite shredded cheese
9-inch deep-dish pie crust
3 eggs, beaten
2/3 c. milk
1 t. salt
1/4 t. pepper

Sauté onion in butter until tender and golden. Spread alternate layers of onions and cheese in pie crust, ending with cheese. Combine remaining ingredients; beat lightly. Pour over onions and cheese. Bake, uncovered, at 450 degrees for 30 minutes. Makes 4 servings.

Mexicali Chicken Stack-Ups

Sue Wright, Killeen, TX

A family favorite! I took a recipe we all enjoyed and tweaked it to include even more ingredients we like...yummy!

4 8-inch flour tortillas, divided
2 boneless, skinless chicken breasts, cooked and diced
  or shredded
3/4 c. salsa
1/4 c. sliced black olives
1 t. ground cumin
1 c. shredded Cheddar cheese, divided
Garnish: sour cream, olives, sliced green onions

Place one tortilla in the bottom of a lightly greased 2-quart round casserole dish; set aside. In a bowl, mix chicken, salsa, olives, cumin and 3/4 cup cheese. Spoon 1/3 of chicken mixture over tortilla in dish. Repeat layering, ending with the last tortilla. Sprinkle with remaining cheese. Cover with aluminum foil. Bake at 350 degrees for 30 to 35 minutes, until hot and bubbly, uncovering for the final 5 minutes. Cut into wedges and garnish with sour cream, olives and sliced green onions. Makes 2 to 4 servings.

Mexicali Chicken Stack-Ups

Mashed Potato Pie

Laurie Kunigel, Schenectady, NY

A one-dish meal that my mom used to make...it always tasted so good after I'd been playing outside in the snow all day!

1 lb. ground beef, browned and drained
10-3/4 oz. can tomato soup
14-1/2 oz. can French-style green beans, drained
2 to 3 c. mashed potatoes

Combine beef, soup and beans in an ungreased 2-quart casserole dish. Spread potatoes over top. Bake, uncovered, at 350 degrees for 20 to 30 minutes, until potatoes are lightly golden. Serves 6.

Saucy Pork Chops

Cindy McCormick, Bakersfield, CA

You'll want to finish every drop of the delicious sauce!

2 10-3/4 oz. cans cream of chicken soup
1/2 c. catsup
6 t. Worcestershire sauce
4 to 6 pork chops
2-1/2 c. cooked rice

Mix together soup, catsup and Worcestershire sauce; set aside. Arrange pork chops in an ungreased 13"x9" baking pan; pour soup mixture over the top. Cover and bake at 350 degrees for one hour. Serve each pork chop on a serving of rice; spoon remaining sauce on top. Serves 4 to 6.

Mom's Cheesy Hashbrowns

Valerie Hendrickson, Cedar Springs, MI

1/4 c. butter
1 sweet onion, chopped
2 c. shredded Cheddar cheese
1 c. sour cream
30-oz. pkg. country-style frozen shredded
   hashbrowns, thawed

Melt butter in a medium saucepan over medium heat. Add onion and cook until translucent, about 5 minutes. Mix in cheese and continue stirring until melted. Remove from heat; stir in sour cream. Gently fold mixture into hashbrowns. Spoon into a greased 2-quart casserole dish. Bake, uncovered, at 350 degrees for 60 to 75 minutes, until heated through and top is golden. Serves 6 to 8.

My mother used to make this scrumptious dish the old-fashioned way, starting with hand-shredded boiled potatoes. This version is simplified using frozen shredded potatoes, yet is still full of hearty homestyle flavor! —Valerie

Mom's Cheesy Hashbrowns

Texas Hominy

Rita Barnett, Lewisburg, TN

I got this recipe from my aunt, who lived in Texas for several years while her husband was stationed there in the Air Force. When my son's school cafeteria asked for recipes to serve to the students, this turned out to be quite popular. My teenage son has often eaten at least half of it in one sitting!

15-1/2 oz. can hominy, drained
15-oz. can chili
2 c. tortilla or corn chips, crushed
1-1/2 to 2 c. shredded Cheddar or Mexican-blend cheese

In a lightly greased 9"x9" baking pan, combine hominy and chili. Top with chips and cheese. Bake, uncovered, at 350 degrees for 25 to 30 minutes, until heated through and cheese melts. Serves 4.

Quick tip

Use individual ramekins or small casserole dishes to bake individual servings of your favorite casserole. It is fun to serve and looks so special!

Family-Favorite Corn Soufflé

Family-Favorite Corn Soufflé

Donna Maltman, Toledo, OH

An absolute must-have for Thanksgiving dinner.

15-oz. can corn, drained
8-1/2 oz. pkg. cornbread mix
14-3/4 oz. can creamed corn
1 c. sour cream
1/4 c. butter, melted
8-oz. pkg. shredded Cheddar cheese

Combine all ingredients except cheese. Pour into a lightly greased 13"x9" baking pan or into 8 lightly greased ramekins. Cover with aluminum foil. Bake at 350 degrees for 30 minutes. Uncover; top with cheese. Return to oven and continue baking until cheese is bubbly and golden, about 15 minutes. Serves 8 to 10.

Family-Favorite Corn Soufflé

Linda's Rigatoni Bake

Celia Day, Cerritos, CA

A dear friend made this yummy casserole for me years ago while I was recovering from surgery. Since then, I have been fixing it for my family...it's their favorite!

16-oz. pkg. rigatoni pasta, uncooked
1 lb. ground beef or ground Italian pork sausage
26-oz. jar pasta sauce, divided
1 c. shredded Monterey Jack cheese
1 c. shredded Cheddar cheese
Garnish: grated Parmesan cheese

Cook pasta according to package directions; drain. Meanwhile, brown meat in a skillet over medium heat; drain. Add pasta sauce, reserving 1/2 cup sauce. Simmer for 10 minutes. Spread reserved sauce in a 13"x9" baking pan coated with non-stick vegetable spray. Layer with half each of pasta, meat sauce and shredded cheeses; repeat layers. Sprinkle Parmesan cheese over top. Bake, uncovered, at 350 degrees for 30 minutes, or until hot and bubbly. Serves 4 to 6.

Penne Sausage Bake

Bev Bornheimer, Lyons, NY

1 lb. hot or mild ground Italian pork sausage
3 cloves garlic, chopped
24-oz. jar marinara sauce with cabernet and herbs
1/2 t. red pepper flakes
1/2 t. salt
1/2 t. pepper
12-oz. pkg. penne pasta, cooked
1 c. shredded mozzarella cheese
Garnish: grated Parmesan cheese, chopped fresh
   parsley

Cook sausage in a skillet over medium heat until browned; drain. Return sausage to pan. Add garlic and cook until tender, about 2 minutes. Stir in sauce and seasonings. Stir sauce mixture into cooked pasta; pour mixture into a greased 12"x8" baking pan. Top with mozzarella cheese. Bake, covered, at 375 degrees for 25 to 30 minutes, until bubbly and cheese has melted. Remove from oven; sprinkle with Parmesan cheese and parsley. Serves 6.

Quick tip

A flexible plastic cutting mat makes speedy work of slicing & dicing. Keep two mats on hand for chopping meat and veggies separately.

Penne Sausage Bake

Cheddar Baked Spaghetti

Carol McKeon, Lebanon, TN

This is my version of a dish my mother often made for us...it was our favorite Friday dinner. My brother and I still love it, as it always reminds us of Mom.

16-oz. pkg. thin spaghetti, uncooked
1/2 c. butter, softened
16-oz. jar double Cheddar cheese pasta sauce
12-oz. can tomato paste
2 T. sugar
1/3 c. Italian-flavored dry bread crumbs

Cook spaghetti according to package directions, just until tender. Drain; return to cooking pot. Add butter; toss spaghetti until butter melts. Stir in pasta sauce, tomato paste and sugar. Transfer to a greased 13"x9" baking pan; sprinkle with bread crumbs. Bake, uncovered, at 350 degrees for 35 minutes, or until bubbly and crunchy on top. Serves 6 to 8.

Cheddar Baked Spaghetti

Chile Relleno Casserole

Gerri Bowers, Farwell, TX

16-oz. pkg. shredded Monterey Jack cheese
16-oz. pkg. shredded Cheddar cheese
2 8-oz. cans whole green chiles
4 eggs, separated
1 T. all-purpose flour
2/3 c. evaporated milk
salt and pepper to taste

Sprinkle both packages of cheese into a lightly greased 13"x9" baking pan. Arrange chiles over cheese; set aside. Beat egg yolks in a bowl; gradually beat in flour and milk. In a separate bowl, beat egg whites until fluffy; stir into yolk mixture. Add salt and pepper to taste. Drizzle egg mixture over chiles. Bake, uncovered, at 325 degrees for 50 minutes. Let stand several minutes before serving. Makes 8 servings.

My mom served this Chile Relleno Casserole when I was a child, and I've always loved it. Serve it with Spanish rice and refried beans...yum! —Gerri

Chile Relleno Casserole

Quick & Easy Quiche

Quick & Easy Quiche

Purchased pie crusts make quiche-making so easy!

1/2 of a 2.8-oz pkg. cooked bacon
9-inch pie crust
8 eggs
8-oz jar creamy blue cheese salad dressing
1 T. fresh parsley, chopped
Garnish: fresh chives

Crumble bacon into pie crust. Blend together eggs, salad dressing and parsley in a large bowl; pour into crust. Bake at 350 degrees for 25 to 30 minutes, or until puffed and a knife inserted in the center comes out clean. Cool on a wire rack for 5 minutes before cutting. Serves 6 to 8.

Daddy's Shepherd's Pie

Sheila Wakeman, Winnsboro, TX

My dad grew up eating this dish. I can remember going to Dad's house on the weekends (he was a single dad) and we would make this together. Now my daughter and I make it together too.

1 lb. ground beef
10-3/4 oz. can cream of mushroom soup
2/3 c. water
7.2-oz. pkg. homestyle creamy butter-flavored instant mashed potato flakes
2 c. frozen corn
8-oz. pkg. shredded Cheddar cheese

Brown beef in a skillet over medium heat; drain. Stir in soup and water; simmer until heated through. Meanwhile, prepare potato flakes as package directs; set aside. Place beef mixture in a 13"x9" baking pan sprayed with non-stick vegetable spray. Top with corn; spread potatoes evenly across top. Sprinkle with cheese. Bake, uncovered, at 425 degrees for about 10 minutes, until hot and cheese is melted. Makes 6 to 8 servings.

White Cheddar-Cauliflower Casserole

Lisa Ashton, Aston, PA

Lots of cheese and bacon will have the kids eating their cauliflower in this terrific casserole.

1 head cauliflower, cooked and mashed
8-oz. pkg. shredded white Cheddar cheese, divided
1/2 lb. bacon, crisply cooked, crumbled and divided
1/2 c. cream cheese, softened
2 T. sour cream
salt and pepper to taste

Combine cauliflower, half the Cheddar cheese and 3/4 of the bacon in a bowl. Add cream cheese and sour cream; mix well. Spread mixture in a greased 8"x8" baking pan; top with remaining Cheddar cheese and bacon. Sprinkle with salt and pepper. Bake, uncovered, at 350 degrees for 20 to 25 minutes, until bubbly and golden around edges. Serves 6.

White Cheddar-Cauliflower Casserole

Golden Macaroni & Cheese

Gale Harris, Fort Worth, TX

A topping of crispy French fried onions gives this traditional standby extra crunch!

10-3/4 oz. can cream of mushroom soup
1/2 c. milk
1/2 t. mustard
1/8 t. pepper
3 c. elbow macaroni, cooked
2 c. shredded Cheddar cheese, divided
1 c. French fried onions

Blend soup, milk, mustard and pepper in a lightly greased 1-1/2 quart casserole dish. Stir in macaroni and 1-1/2 cups cheese. Bake, uncovered, at 350 degrees for 20 minutes. Top with remaining cheese and onions; bake 10 additional minutes. Serves 4.

Quick tip

You can make your own stuffing mix by toasting bread, cutting the bread into cubes and adding your favorite seasonings. Keep in plastic bags in the freezer until ready to use.

Mimi's Stuffed Pork Chops

Mori Green, Conroe, TX

6-oz. pkg. pork or chicken flavored stuffing mix
1 c. yellow onion, chopped
1 red pepper, chopped
1/4 c. butter, divided
6 boneless pork chops, 1-inch thick
12-oz. jar turkey gravy, or 1 c. homemade gravy, warmed

Prepare stuffing mix as package directs. Meanwhile, in a small skillet over medium heat, cook onion and red pepper in 2 tablespoons butter until onion is tender. Stir onion mixture into prepared stuffing. With a sharp knife, cut into the side of each pork chop to form a pocket. Brown in 2 tablespoons butter on both sides. Scoop 2 spoonfuls of stuffing into each pork chop. Place stuffed pork chops in a 2-quart casserole dish; spoon any remaining stuffing around pork chops. Bake, uncovered at 350 degrees for 30 to 40 minutes until pork chops are tender. Serve with warmed gravy. Makes 6 servings.

I love making this recipe for a special weeknight dinner or a Sunday lunch. It is one of my family's favorites. —Mori

Mimi's Stuffed Pork Chops

Summer Squash Pie

Summer Squash Pie

Kelly Patrick, Ashburn, VA

3 c. yellow squash, peeled and diced
1/2 c. onion, chopped
4 eggs, beaten
1/3 c. canola oil
1 c. biscuit baking mix
1/2 c. shredded mozzarella cheese
salt and pepper to taste

Mix all ingredients in a bowl. Pat into a 9" pie plate lightly coated with non-stick vegetable spray. Bake at 350 degrees for 50 minutes to one hour, until set. Let stand for 10 minutes; slice into wedges. Serve warm or cold. Makes 6 to 8 servings.

My mother and I have used this recipe every summer when summer squash is abundant. It's a very simple, one-bowl recipe that takes literally five minutes to toss together... it's never failed us! Feel free to try different cheeses or add your favorite chopped veggies. —Kelly

Poor Man's Steak & Vegetables

Cynthia Armstrong, Big Stone Gap, VA

This recipe has been handed down for several generations. My mother used to serve this dish when money was tight. It has become a family favorite!

6 ground beef patties
4 potatoes, peeled and cubed
3 carrots, peeled and diced
1 onion, quartered or sliced
salt and pepper to taste

Place patties in a greased 13"x9" baking pan. Evenly arrange vegetables over patties. Sprinkle with salt and pepper to taste. Bake, covered, at 400 degrees for 45 to 50 minutes, or until beef is no longer pink and potatoes are tender. Serves 6.

Poor Man's Steak & Vegetables

Cheeseburger Bake

Cheeseburger Bake

Jennifer Williams, Los Angeles, CA

This hearty meal is great after a long day of work and errands...so filling.

8-oz. tube refrigerated crescent rolls
1 lb. ground beef
1-1/4 oz. pkg. taco seasoning mix
15-oz. can tomato sauce
2 c. shredded Cheddar cheese
Garnish: chopped green onions

Unroll crescent roll dough; separate triangles and press into a greased 9" round baking pan, pinching seams closed. Bake at 350 degrees for 10 minutes; set aside. Meanwhile, brown beef in a skillet over medium heat; drain. Add taco seasoning and sauce; heat through. Spoon over crescent rolls and sprinkle cheese on top. Bake, uncovered, for 10 to 15 minutes. Let stand 5 minutes before serving. Garnish with chopped green onions. Serves 4.

Quick tip

Don't toss out the last cheese crackers or potato chips in the bag. Crush them and use them to add to meatloaf or for casserole toppings.

Broccoli Supreme

Linda Belon, Wintersville, OH

A delicious side that whips up in a jiffy! Serve with a sandwich for a complete meal.

1 egg, beaten
10-oz. pkg. frozen chopped broccoli, partially thawed and drained
8-1/2 oz. can creamed corn
1 T. onion, grated
1/4 t. salt
1/8 t. pepper
1 c. herb-flavored stuffing mix
3 T. butter, melted

In a bowl, combine egg, broccoli, corn, onion, salt and pepper. In a separate bowl, toss stuffing mix with butter. Stir 3/4 cup of stuffing mixture into egg mixture. Turn into an ungreased 8"x8" baking pan. Sprinkle with remaining stuffing mixture. Bake, uncovered, at 350 degrees for 35 to 40 minutes, until bubbly. Makes 6 to 8 servings.

Broccoli Supreme

Pop-in-the-Oven Casseroles & Quiches

Easy-As-1-2-3 Chicken Bake

Barbara Bower, Orrville, OH

Serve with steamed broccoli or asparagus.

3/4 c. corn flake cereal, crushed
3/4 c. grated Parmesan cheese
1-oz. pkg. Italian salad dressing mix
8 boneless, skinless chicken breasts
1/3 c. butter, melted

Mix cereal, Parmesan cheese and salad dressing mix together; coat chicken. Place in a single layer in a greased 13"x9" baking pan. Sprinkle remaining crumbs on top; drizzle with butter. Bake at 350 degrees for 45 minutes or until juices run clear when chicken is pierced with a fork. Serves 8.

Quick & Easy Lasagna

Tina Stuart, Scottsdale, AZ

Extra cheesy, this lasagna's a winner!

1 lb. ground beef, browned
2 24-oz. jars pasta sauce
16-oz. pkg. lasagna noodles, cooked and divided
2 c. ricotta cheese, divided
16-oz. pkg. shredded mozzarella cheese, divided

Mix together ground beef and pasta sauce; set aside. Spread one cup pasta sauce mixture in bottom of an ungreased 13"x9" baking pan, laying with about half the noodles. Pour half the remaining sauce on top; drop half the ricotta cheese by spoonfuls onto the sauce. Sprinkle with half the mozzarella cheese; repeat layers, beginning with the noodles. Bake, uncovered, at 350 degrees for 30 to 35 minutes or until cheese melts. Serves 12.

Meatball-Stuffed Shells

Jenny Bishoff, Mountain Lake Park, MD

As a working mom with two little girls, I've found this super-easy recipe is great for a quick dinner. The kids can help too!

12-oz. pkg. jumbo pasta shells, uncooked
28-oz. jar pasta sauce, divided
36 frozen Italian meatballs, thawed
2 c. shredded mozzarella cheese
Garnish: grated Parmesan cheese

Cook pasta according to package directions; drain and rinse in cold water. Spread 1/2 cup pasta sauce in a greased 13"x9" baking pan. Tuck a meatball into each shell; arrange shells in pan. Top with remaining sauce; add cheese. Cover; bake at 350 degrees for 35 minutes. Uncover and bake 10 more minutes. Serves 6 to 8.

Yummy Pork Ribs

Lee Beedle, Church View, VA

I enjoy trying new recipes and this is one I find myself recommending to everyone...it's delectable and oh-so-easy!

2 c. zesty Italian salad dressing
1/4 c. soy sauce
1 T. garlic, minced
1/2 t. pepper
3 to 4 lbs. bone-in country-style pork ribs or chops
2 T. olive oil
2 to 3 onions, sliced into rings

In a small bowl, stir together salad dressing, soy sauce, garlic and pepper; set aside. In a skillet over medium heat, brown ribs in oil on both sides; drain. Arrange onion rings in an ungreased 13"x9" baking pan. Top with ribs; drizzle dressing mixture over top. Cover tightly. Bake at 350 degrees for one hour, or until tender. Serves 6.

Meatball-Stuffed Shells

Hashbrown Casserole

Shelia Butts, Creedmoor, NC

Such a creamy, filling side dish and it's so easy to make.

10-3/4 oz. can cream of chicken soup
8-oz. container sour cream
1/2 c. margarine, melted and divided
2 c. shredded sharp Cheddar cheese
salt and pepper to taste
30-oz. pkg. frozen shredded hashbrowns, thawed
1 c. corn flake cereal, crushed

In a bowl, combine soup, sour cream, half the margarine, shredded cheese, salt and pepper. Pour mixture into a lightly greased 13"x9" baking pan; top with hashbrowns. Mix corn flake cereal and remaining margarine; spread over hashbrowns. Bake, uncovered, at 350 degrees for 30 minutes, or until hot and bubbly. Serves 6.

Hashbrown Casserole

Tamale Pie

Kelly Cook, Dunedin, FL

Ready-made tamales make this pie oh-so-quick.

2 15-oz. cans beef tamales, divided
15-oz. can chili, divided
9-1/4 oz. pkg. corn chips, divided
1 onion, minced and divided
2 c. shredded Cheddar cheese, divided

Chop one can of tamales; set aside. Spread one cup chili in the bottom of a greased 2-quart casserole dish; layer half the corn chips, half the onion and chopped tamales on top. Sprinkle with half the cheese; repeat layers, ending with whole tamales topped with cheese. Cover and bake at 350 degrees for one hour. Let cool for 10 minutes before serving. Serves 12.

Mustard Chicken

Joy Collins, Vestavia, AL

This dish is easy and delicious! If I haven't made it for awhile, my husband will ask for it. It's easy to double or even triple if you're hosting a crowd or going to a potluck.

1/2 c. mayonnaise
1/2 c. butter, melted and slightly cooled
3 T. mustard
6-oz. pkg. herb-flavored stuffing mix
8 boneless, skinless chicken breasts

Mix together mayonnaise, butter and mustard in a shallow bowl. Place dry stuffing mix in a separate shallow bowl. Add chicken to mayonnaise mixture; coat well. Dip chicken into stuffing mix and press on both sides to coat. Arrange chicken in a lightly greased 13"x9" baking pan. Bake, covered, at 350 degrees for one hour. Uncover; bake for another 30 minutes, or until chicken juices run clear. Makes 8 servings.

Tamale Pie

Cheesy Chile Rice

Cheesy Chile Rice

Wendy Reaume, Ontario, Canada

When I was growing up, my mom made this simple rice dish whenever we had Mexican food for dinner. It's yummy with burritos and tortilla chips.

2 c. water
2 c. instant rice, uncooked
16-oz. container sour cream
4-oz. can diced green chiles
3 c. shredded Cheddar cheese, divided

In a saucepan over medium-high heat, bring water to a boil. Stir in rice; remove from heat. Cover and let stand 5 minutes, until water is absorbed. In a large bowl, mix together rice, sour cream, chiles and 2 cups cheese. Spread in a greased 2-quart casserole dish; top with remaining cheese. Bake, uncovered, at 400 degrees for 30 minutes, or until cheese is melted and top is lightly golden. Makes 6 servings.

Beef & Cheddar Quiche

Dianne Young, South Jordan, UT

So tasty topped with sour cream or even salsa!

3 eggs, beaten
1 c. whipping cream
1 c. shredded Cheddar cheese
1 c. ground beef, browned
9-inch pie crust

Mix eggs, cream, cheese and beef together; spread into pie crust. Bake at 450 degrees for 15 minutes; lower oven temperature to 350 degrees and continue baking for 15 minutes. Serves 8.

Beef & Cheddar Quiche

Egg Casserole Deluxe

Egg Casserole Deluxe

Natasha Morris, Ulysses, KS

1 to 2 T. butter
1/2 cup sliced mushrooms
1 doz. eggs, beaten
8-oz. container sour cream
1/2 c. shredded Cheddar cheese
2.8-oz. pkg. pre-cooked bacon, crumbled and divided

Melt butter in a large skillet over medium heat. Sauté mushrooms. Add eggs; cook and stir until softly scrambled. Stir in sour cream, mushrooms, cheese and half of bacon. Transfer to a lightly greased 8"x8" baking pan. Sprinkle remaining bacon on top. Bake, uncovered, at 350 degrees for 30 minutes. Serves 8.

This recipe is so versatile! My youngest daughter made this for her sister's bridal shower...it was a big hit with the bride-to-be and the guests! For a crowd, simply double the recipe and bake in a 13"x9" baking pan. For a quick weeknight dinner, just add a fruit salad and dinner is done! —Natasha

French Toast Casserole

French Toast Casserole

Lori Hurley, Fishers, IN

A really simple way to make French toast for a crowd. Pop it in the fridge the night before, then all you have to do is bake it the next day. Serve with bacon for a great dinner!

1 c. brown sugar, packed
1/2 c. butter
2 c. corn syrup
1 loaf French bread, sliced
5 eggs, beaten
1-1/2 c. milk
Garnish: powdered sugar, maple syrup

Melt together brown sugar, butter and corn syrup in a saucepan over low heat; pour into a greased 13"x9" baking pan. Arrange bread slices over mixture and set aside. Whisk together eggs and milk; pour over bread, coating all slices. Cover and refrigerate overnight. Uncover and bake at 350 degrees for 30 minutes, or until lightly golden. Sprinkle with powdered sugar; serve with warm syrup. Makes 6 to 8 servings.

Savory Rice Casserole

Savory Rice Casserole

Kathy Dassel, Newburgh, IN

My sister-in-law gave me this delicious recipe while we were visiting her in Raleigh, North Carolina.

4-oz. can sliced mushrooms, drained and liquid reserved
8-oz. can sliced water chestnuts, drained and liquid reserved
1/2 c. butter
1 c. long-cooking rice, uncooked
10-1/2 oz. can French onion soup

In a skillet over medium heat, sauté mushrooms and water chestnuts in butter; set aside. Add uncooked rice to an ungreased one-quart casserole dish. Stir in soup, mushroom mixture and reserved liquids. Bake, covered, at 375 degrees for 45 to 60 minutes, until rice is tender. Serves 6 to 8.

Spicy Chicken Casserole

Martha Stephens, Sibley, LA

A hearty, creamy dinner in one dish...with just four ingredients!

4 to 5 boneless, skinless chicken breasts
2 10-3/4 oz. cans cream of chicken soup
2 10-3/4 oz. cans nacho cheese soup
3 to 4 c. tortilla chips, crushed and divided

Cover chicken breasts with water in a large saucepan. Simmer over medium-high heat just until cooked through. Drain, saving broth for another use. Cool chicken slightly; shred into bite-size pieces, and set aside. Combine soups in a saucepan. Stir well; cook over medium heat until bubbly. Remove from heat. In a greased 13"x9" baking pan, layer half of chicken, half of soup mixture and half of the crushed chips. Repeat layers. Cover and bake at 350 degrees for 20 minutes or until heated through. Serves 6.

Easy Chicken Pot Pie

Lynne Gasior, Struthers, OH

This is also a great way to use up leftover chicken or a rotisserie chicken.

2 8-oz. cans chicken, drained
2 13-1/4 oz. cans mixed vegetables, drained
2 10-3/4 oz. cans cream of chicken soup
1 c. milk
salt and pepper to taste
8-oz. pkg. shredded Cheddar or Colby cheese, divided
12-oz. tube refrigerated biscuits

In a bowl, combine all ingredients except cheese and biscuits. Transfer to a greased 13"x9" baking pan; top with 3/4 of cheese. Separate biscuits and tear each into 4 to 5 pieces; place on top of cheese. Sprinkle with remaining cheese. Bake, uncovered, at 350 degrees for 45 minutes, or until biscuits are golden. Serves 4.

Spicy Chicken Casserole

Chicken & Rice Casserole

Chicken & Rice Casserole

Kimberly Lyons, Commerce, TX

Great with fresh-baked bread and a green salad.

2 6.2-oz. pkgs. quick-cooking long-grain and wild rice
   with seasoning packets
4 boneless, skinless chicken breasts, cooked and cut
   into 1" cubes
3 10-3/4 oz. can cream of mushroom soup
1-1/3 c. frozen mixed vegetables, thawed
3 c. water

Gently stir together all ingredients. Spread into an
ungreased 13"x9" baking pan. Bake, uncovered, at
350 degrees about 45 minutes, stirring occasionally.
Serves 6 to 8.

Green Bean Baked Lucette

Bethany Zemaitis, Pittsburgh, PA

*My husband's grandmother introduced me to this yummy
green bean casserole. Now, it's often requested by my friends
& family.*

2 14-1/2 oz. cans green beans, drained and 1/4 c. liquid
   reserved
2 6-oz. cans French fried onions, divided
3/4 c. shredded Cheddar cheese
10-3/4 oz. can cream of mushroom soup

In a lightly greased 2-quart casserole dish, alternate
layers of green beans, 1 c. onions and cheese. Mix soup
and reserved liquid in a separate bowl; pour over bean
mixture. Sprinkle remaining onions over casserole. Bake,
uncovered, at 325 degrees for about 40 minutes. Serves
6 to 8.

Denver Oven Omelet

Charlene McCain, Bakersfield, CA

*Delicious and easy! I have taken this simple dish to many
potlucks. My family even enjoys it on busy weeknights too.*

8 eggs, beaten
1/2 c. half-and-half
1 c. shredded Cheddar cheese
1 c. cooked ham, chopped
1/4 c. green pepper, chopped
1/4 c. onion, finely chopped
salt and pepper to taste

In a large bowl, whisk eggs and half-and-half until
light and fluffy. Stir in remaining ingredients. Pour
into a greased 9"x9" baking pan. Bake, uncovered,
at 400 degrees for 25 minutes, or until set and golden.
Serves 4.

Quick tip

If you need a new casserole dish, consider
getting a deep 13"x9" glass baking dish.
It retains heat well to create crisp golden
crusts, cleans up easily and can be used for
both casseroles and desserts.

7

Stovetop Skillet Dinners

(simple & satisfying)

What could be better than a one-pan dinner? Go from stovetop to tabletop in no time with these 6-ingredient one-skillet meals! South-of-the-Border Squash Skillet goes together quickly and tastes so yummy! Serve Beef Porcupine Meatballs with cooked noodles for a complete meal that they'll all enjoy! Switch it up a little with a Curried Chicken with Mango that you make in a skillet. No matter what recipe you choose, you'll all agree that a flash in the pan can be a good thing!

Inside-Out Stuffed Pepper

Charlene McCain, Bakersfield, CA

A quick and tasty dish for those nights when you get home late and everybody's hungry...super-simple to toss together and satisfies even the biggest of hungers!

1 green pepper, top removed
1 lb. ground beef
1 onion, chopped
1-1/2 c. cooked rice
8-oz. can tomato sauce
salt and pepper to taste

Bring a saucepan of salted water to a boil. Add green pepper and cook for 8 to 10 minutes, until tender. Drain; cool slightly and chop pepper. Meanwhile, cook beef and onion in a skillet over medium heat, stirring often, until beef is browned and onion is translucent. Drain; add green pepper and cooked rice to skillet. Pour tomato sauce over beef mixture; stir and heat through. Season with salt and pepper to taste. Serves 4.

Inside-Out Stuffed Pepper

Lemon Wine Chicken Skillet

Judy Young, Plano, TX

This is one of my family's all-time favorite chicken recipes. It is so easy to make and tastes phenomenal! Serve with steamed brown rice or pasta.

4 boneless, skinless chicken breasts
lemon pepper to taste
1 egg
1/2 c. lemon-flavored white cooking wine, divided
1/4 c. all-purpose flour
6 T. butter, divided
2 to 3 T. capers
Garnish: chopped fresh parsley

Flatten chicken breasts slightly between 2 pieces of wax paper. Season chicken with lemon pepper. In a small bowl, lightly beat egg with 2 tablespoons wine. Place flour in a separate shallow bowl. Dip chicken in egg mixture, then in flour to coat. Melt 3 tablespoons butter in a large skillet over medium heat; add chicken. Cook until golden on both sides and no longer pink in the center, about 6 minutes on each side. Transfer chicken to a serving dish. Add remaining wine and butter to drippings in skillet; cook and stir until butter melts. Add capers; heat through. To serve, spoon sauce from the skillet over chicken; sprinkle with parsley. Serves 4.

Quick tip

When freezing leftover diced peppers, corn or fresh herbs, add a little olive oil to the plastic zipping bag. It will keep the food separated and fresher too.

Lemon Wine Chicken Skillet

Stovetop Skillet Dinners

Mom's Cola Chicken

Carla Slajchert, St. Petersburg, FL

Growing up, we knew Mom would be making this delicious, tender chicken whenever we saw her get out the skillet.

1 to 2 T. oil
1-1/2 lbs. boneless, skinless chicken breasts
salt and pepper to taste
20-oz. bottle cola, divided
1 to 2 c. catsup, divided

Heat oil in a large skillet over medium heat. Add chicken to oil; sprinkle with salt and pepper and brown on both sides. Pour enough cola into skillet to cover chicken. Slowly add enough catsup to skillet until mixture reaches desired thickness. Cover and cook over medium heat for about 45 minutes, adding remaining cola and catsup, a little at a time, every 10 to 15 minutes, until chicken juices run clear. Serves 4.

Beef & Noodle Skillet

Angie Dixon, Pevely, MO

Hearty and zesty to warm your tummy.

1 lb. ground beef, browned
2 10-1/2 oz. cans beef broth
8-oz. pkg. elbow macaroni
16-oz. pkg. pasteurized process cheese spread, cubed
1 c. salsa

Place beef in a 12" skillet; add broth. Heat to boiling; stir in macaroni. Boil until macaroni is tender; reduce heat and mix in cheese and salsa. Heat through, stirring occasionally. Serves 4.

Beef Porcupine Meatballs

Terri Lock, Carrollton, MO

8-oz. pkg. beef-flavored rice vermicelli mix
1 lb. ground beef
1 egg, beaten
2-1/2 c. water
cooked egg noodles

In a bowl, combine rice vermicelli mix, beef and egg, reserving seasoning packet from mix. Form mixture into one-inch balls. In a skillet over medium heat, cook meatballs, turning occasionally, until browned on all sides; drain. In a bowl, combine seasoning packet and water; pour over meatballs. Cover and simmer for 30 minutes, or until thickened and meatballs are no longer pink in the center. Serve meatballs and sauce over noodles. Makes 4 to 6 servings.

As a teacher, I need fast homestyle meals to serve to my family of five before I leave for evening school events...this recipe is perfect. —Terri

Beef Porcupine Meatballs

Family Favorite Chili Mac

Buttermilk Fried Chicken

Cyndi Little, Whitsett, NC

2-1/2 lbs. chicken, cut up
1 c. buttermilk
1 c. all-purpose flour
1-1/2 t. salt
1/2 t. pepper
oil for frying

Combine chicken and buttermilk in a large bowl. Cover and refrigerate for one hour. Meanwhile, combine flour, salt and pepper in a large plastic zipping bag. Drain chicken, discarding buttermilk. Working in batches, add chicken to bag and toss to coat. Shake off excess flour and let chicken rest for 15 minutes. Heat 1/4 inch of oil in a large skillet over medium heat. Fry chicken in oil until golden on all sides. Reduce heat to medium-low; cover and simmer, turning occasionally, for 40 to 45 minutes, until juices run clear. Uncover and cook 5 minutes longer. Serves 4 to 6.

Family Favorite Chili Mac

Stephanie McNealy, Talala, OK

Kids love this quick & easy dinner. Serve with a tossed salad and cornbread sticks.

2 7-1/4 oz. pkgs. macaroni & cheese
10-oz. can diced tomatoes and green chiles
1 to 2 lbs. ground beef
1-1/4 oz. pkg. taco seasoning mix
chili power, salt and pepper to taste

Prepare macaroni and cheese according to package directions. Stir in tomatoes and green chiles; set aside. Brown beef in a skillet; drain and mix in taco seasoning. Stir beef mixture into macaroni mixture. Add seasonings as desired; heat through. Serves 7 to 9.

My daddy made amazing fried chicken! He is gone now, and it has taken me a long time to make chicken that I feel is almost as good as his. This recipe is so wonderful with the crunchy buttermilk batter. —Cyndi

Buttermilk Fried Chicken

Roasted Tomato-Feta Broccoli

Heat oil in a skillet over medium heat. Add broccoli, tomatoes, lemon juice and seasonings; cook until vegetables are crisp-tender. Transfer warm vegetable mixture to a large bowl and mix in cheese. Drizzle with additional olive oil, if desired. Serves 2 to 4.

Festive Brunch Frittata

Renae Scheiderer, Beallsville, OH

8 eggs, beaten
1/2 t. salt
1/8 t. pepper
1/2 c. shredded Cheddar cheese
2 T. butter
2 c. red, green and yellow peppers, chopped
1/4 c. onion, chopped
Garnish: chopped fresh parsley

Beat together eggs, salt and pepper. Fold in Cheddar cheese and set aside. Melt butter over medium heat in a 10" non-stick, oven-safe skillet. Add peppers and onion to skillet; sauté until tender. Pour eggs over peppers and onion; don't stir. Cover and cook over medium-low heat for about 9 minutes. Eggs are set when frittata is lightly golden on the underside. Turn oven on broil. Move skillet from stovetop to oven; broil top about 5 inches from heat until lightly golden. Garnish with parsley. Serves 6.

Roasted Tomato-Feta Broccoli

Lyuba Brooke, Jacksonville, FL

This is such a simple and fast side. Don't let the easiness of it fool you...this dish is full of flavor and it's really healthy.

2 T. olive oil
2 c. broccoli flowerets
1 c. cherry tomatoes
1 t. lemon juice
dried parsley, salt and pepper to taste
1/2 c. crumbled feta cheese
Optional: additional olive oil

An easy, gourmet meal that will impress your family or your guests...also try it with mushrooms and spinach. Change it up to suit your family's favorite flavors. —Renae

Festive Brunch Frittata

Simple Skillet Peaches

Tina Wright, Atlanta, GA

These peaches are delicious on just about anything you can think of. Cereal, oatmeal, ice cream, cobbler...or use them to top big slices of angel food cake!

6 c. peaches, peeled, pitted and cut into bite-size pieces
1/2 c. sugar
1 T. vanilla extract

Combine peaches and sugar in a large skillet over medium heat. Bring to a boil; reduce heat to medium-low. Simmer until peaches are soft and mixture has thickened, about 20 to 25 minutes. Stir in extract. Serve warm or store in an airtight container in the refrigerator. Makes about 6 servings.

Simple Skillet Peaches

Rosemary Peppers & Fusilli

Jennifer Niemi, Nova Scotia, Canada

This colorful, flavorful meatless meal is ready to serve in a jiffy. If you can't find fusilli pasta, try medium shells, rotini or even wagon wheels.

2 to 4 T. olive oil
2 red onions, thinly sliced and separated into rings
3 red, orange and/or yellow peppers, very thinly sliced
5 to 6 cloves garlic, very thinly sliced
3 t. dried rosemary
salt and pepper to taste
12-oz. pkg. fusilli pasta, cooked
Optional: shredded mozzarella cheese

Add oil to a large skillet over medium heat. Add onions to skillet; cover and cook over medium heat for 10 minutes. Stir in remaining ingredients except pasta and cheese; reduce heat. Cook, covered, stirring occasionally, for an additional 20 minutes. Serve vegetable mixture over pasta, topped with cheese if desired. Makes 4 servings.

Ham Frittata

Irene Robinson, Cincinnati, OH

My family loves this quick, filling dish for dinner. It's a great way to use up leftover ham.

1 T. butter
1 c. cooked ham, diced
1/2 c. onion, chopped
1/4 c. green pepper, chopped
4 eggs, beaten
salt and pepper to taste

Melt butter in a microwave-safe bowl; add ham, onion and green pepper. Cover; microwave on high for 2 minutes. Stir in eggs, salt and pepper; microwave on high for an additional 1-1/2 to 2-1/2 minutes. Let stand 3 minutes or until completely set. Serves 2 to 4.

Rosemary Peppers & Fusilli

Pork Chops Olé

Julie De Fusco, Las Vegas, NV

This was one of my favorite dishes to make when I was just learning to cook...it's so easy and so tasty. Make it spicier by adding a little chopped jalapeño.

2 T. oil
4 pork chops
2 T. butter
6.8-oz. pkg. Spanish-flavored rice vermicelli mix
14-1/2 oz. can Mexican-style stewed tomatoes
1-1/2 c. water
Garnish: sour cream, chopped fresh cilantro

Heat oil in a large skillet over medium heat. Cook pork chops in oil until browned on both sides, about 6 minutes; remove from skillet and keep warm. Melt butter in same skillet; add rice mix to butter. Cook and stir until rice mix is lightly golden. Stir in tomatoes with juice and water. Add pork chops to skillet and bring to a boil. Reduce heat to low; cover and cook for 20 to 30 minutes, until liquid is absorbed and pork chops are no longer pink in the center. Garnish with sour cream and cilantro. Serves 4.

Skillet Apples & Pork Chops

Devi McDonald, Visalia, CA

Juicy pan-seared pork chops are paired with sautéed apples and onion...very satisfying.

6 bone-in pork chops
salt and pepper to taste
1/4 c. butter, divided
3 to 4 Granny Smith apples, cored and thinly sliced
1 onion, thinly sliced
1/2 t. fresh thyme, chopped
1 c. lager-style beer or apple cider

Season pork chops with salt and pepper. Melt half of butter in a skillet over medium-high heat. Add pork chops to skillet; cook for 5 minutes. Turn chops over and cook for another 4 minutes, or until juices run clear. Drain; remove chops to a plate. Reduce heat to medium; add remaining butter, apples, onion and thyme to skillet. Cook for about 6 minutes, stirring occasionally; add beer or cider. Cook an additional 15 minutes, or until liquid has reduced and thickened. Return chops to skillet; cover with apple mixture. Cook for 5 minutes. Serve chops topped with apple mixture. Makes 6 servings.

Anita's Onion Steaks

Anita Mullins, Eldridge, MO

A simply delicious way to fix budget-friendly cube steaks! Serve them with mashed potatoes, cooked egg noodles or rice, with the gravy from the skillet ladled over all.

15-oz. can beef broth
Optional: 1/2 c. red wine
1.35-oz. pkg. onion soup mix
1 onion, thinly sliced
4 beef cube steaks
pepper to taste
10-3/4 oz. can cream of onion soup

In a skillet over medium heat, combine broth, wine, if using, and soup mix; mix well. Add onion and steaks; sprinkle with pepper to taste. Reduce heat to low; cover and simmer for 30 minutes. Turn steaks over; cover and simmer for an additional 30 minutes. Remove steaks to a plate; stir soup into mixture in skillet. Return steaks to skillet, being sure to coat each steak with gravy. Cover and simmer over low heat for 15 minutes. Serves 4.

Anita's Onion Steaks

Breezy Brunch Skillet

Breezy Brunch Skillet

Jill Ross, Pickerington, OH

This one-skillet meal is a snap to toss together and the results are scrumptious. I'll often cook this up for dinner, it's so good!

6 slices bacon, diced
6 c. frozen diced potatoes
3/4 c. green pepper, chopped
1/2 c. onion, chopped
1 t. salt
1/4 t. pepper
6 eggs
1/2 c. shredded Cheddar cheese

In a large skillet over medium heat, cook bacon until crisp. Drain and set aside, reserving 2 tablespoons drippings. In the same skillet, add potatoes, green pepper, onion, salt and pepper to drippings. Cook and stir for 2 minutes. Cover and cook for about 15 minutes, stirring occasionally, until potatoes are golden and tender. With a spoon, make 6 wells in potato mixture. Crack one egg into each well, taking care not to break the yolks. Cover and cook on low heat for 8 to 10 minutes, until eggs are completely set. Sprinkle with cheese and bacon. Serves 4 to 6.

Chicken Spaghetti

Glenna Martin, Uwchland, PA

An old family favorite!

1 lb. boneless, skinless chicken breasts, cut into
   bite-size pieces
1/4 c. butter
1 onion, chopped
8-oz. can sliced mushrooms, drained
16-oz. pkg. broccoli flowerets
salt and pepper to taste
16-oz. pkg. spaghetti, cooked
Garnish: grated Parmesan cheese

In a large skillet, sauté chicken in butter until no longer pink. Add onion, mushrooms and broccoli; sauté until chicken is cooked through and vegetables are tender. Add salt and pepper to taste; toss with cooked spaghetti. Sprinkle with Parmesan cheese. Serves 4.

Country Pork Skillet

Lynda Robson, Boston, MA

This one-pot meal is on the table in less than 30 minutes. It's as good as it is easy...even my two picky boys will eat veggies this way!

4 boneless pork chops, diced
1 T. oil
12-oz. jar pork gravy
2 T. catsup
8 new redskin potatoes, diced
2 c. frozen mixed vegetables

In a skillet over medium heat, brown pork in oil; drain. Stir in gravy, catsup and potatoes; cover and simmer for 10 minutes. Stir in vegetables; cook an additional 10 to 15 minutes, until vegetables are tender. Serves 4.

Chicken Spaghetti

Curried Chicken with Mango

Curried Chicken with Mango

Cecilia Ollivares, Santa Paula, CA

2 T. oil
4 boneless, skinless chicken breasts, cooked and sliced
13.6-oz. can coconut milk
1 c. mango, peeled, pitted and cubed
2 to 3 T. curry powder
cooked jasmine rice

Heat oil in a large skillet over medium heat. Cook chicken in oil until golden and warmed through. Stir in milk, mango and curry powder. Simmer for 10 minutes, stirring occasionally, or until slightly thickened. Serve over rice. Serves 4 to 6.

I love dishes like this yummy Curried Chicken with Mango that don't take too long to make and have a unique flavor. This recipe is delicious and speedy...perfect served with a side of naan flatbread. —Cecilia

Ground Beef & Kale Curry

Shannon Hildebrandt, Ontario, Canada

1 lb. ground beef
1/2 c. onion, chopped
3 cloves garlic, minced
28-oz. can diced tomatoes
1 bunch fresh kale, torn and stalks removed
1/2 to 1 T. hot Madras curry powder
salt and pepper to taste
Optional: cooked basmati rice or couscous

In a large skillet over medium heat, cook beef, onion and garlic until beef is no longer pink. Stir in tomatoes with juice and kale; add desired amount of curry powder. Reduce heat to low. Cover and simmer for about 15 minutes, stirring occasionally. Season with salt and pepper. Serve plain or over cooked basmati rice or couscous. Serves 4.

Broccoli Beef Stir-Fry

Diana Chaney, Olathe, KS

My son likes the taste of Chinese pepper steak, but won't eat the green peppers so now I make it with broccoli instead.

.87-oz. pkg. brown gravy mix
1 c. water
1/4 t. pepper
1 T. oil
3/4 to 1 lb. beef flank steak, sliced into thin strips
2 c. broccoli, cut into bite-size flowerets
cooked rice or linguine pasta
Optional: soy sauce

Whisk together gravy mix, water and pepper in a bowl; set aside. Heat oil in a large skillet over medium-high heat. Add beef strips; cook and stir for 3 to 4 minutes. Stir in broccoli and gravy; bring to a boil. Reduce heat to low; cover and simmer 5 to 8 minutes, or until broccoli is crisp-tender. Serve over cooked rice or pasta, with soy sauce if desired. Makes 4 servings.

Stovetop Skillet Dinners

Spicy Sausage & Rice

Brian Johnson, Gastonia, NC

This spicy sausage dish is quick to make on busy evenings after a long day.

3-1/2 c. cooked rice
16-oz. pkg. smoked sausage links, sliced into bite-size
  pieces
8-oz. jar salsa
Garnish: diced green pepper, diced tomato, sliced
  jalapeños

In a large skillet over medium heat, combine all ingredients except garnish. Cook, stirring occasionally, until sausage is heated through and most of the liquid is absorbed. Top servings with diced pepper, diced tomato and jalapeño slices. Makes 6 to 8 servings.

Santa Fe Chicken & Potatoes

Tina George, El Dorado, AR

This five-ingredient recipe is simple to prepare on busy nights when you're pressed for time! It smells so good when it's cooking, and it's easy to double for my large family. My family loves this dish served with sweet cornbread muffins.

4 potatoes, peeled and cut into 3/4-inch cubes
1 lb. boneless, skinless chicken breasts, cut into
  3/4-inch cubes
2 T. olive oil
1 c. salsa
11-oz. can corn, drained

Place potatoes in a microwave-safe dish; add a small amount of water. Cover with plastic wrap; vent and microwave on high for 8 to 10 minutes, until tender. Meanwhile, in a large skillet over high heat, sauté chicken in oil over medium-high heat for 5 minutes. Add potatoes; sauté and toss until potatoes are lightly golden. Stir in salsa and corn; toss until heated through. Serves 4.

Spicy Sausage & Rice

Olive & Feta Cheese Omelet

Holly Jackson, Saint George, UT

All I can say is, "Mmm!"

2 eggs, beaten
1/4 c. crumbled feta cheese
1/4 c. cucumber, diced
2 T. green onion, chopped
1/4 c. cooked ham, cubed
salt and pepper to taste
Garnish: salsa

Combine all ingredients except salsa in a bowl; mix well. Pour into a lightly greased sauté pan or small skillet. Without stirring, cook over low heat until set. Fold over; transfer to serving plate. Serve with salsa. Makes one serving.

Olive & Feta Cheese Omelet

Tempting Teriyaki Chicken

Amy Holt, Enterprise, UT

I have to triple this recipe when I make it for my family...they absolutely love it.

2/3 c. soy sauce
1/3 c. sugar
1/4 t. ground ginger
1/8 t. garlic powder
4 to 5 boneless, skinless chicken breasts
cooked rice
Garnish: sliced green onions, sesame seed

In a large skillet over medium heat, whisk together soy sauce, sugar, ginger and garlic powder. When heated through, add chicken. Cover and simmer, basting chicken occasionally with sauce, for about 30 minutes, until chicken is no longer pink in the center. Uncover and cook an additional 10 minutes, or until sauce thickens. Serve with rice; garnish with green onions and sesame seed. Serves 4 to 6.

Tempting Teriyaki Chicken

South-of-the-Border Squash Skillet

Brenda Rogers, Atwood, CA

Our family grows lots of yellow summer squash in our community garden. We love tacos, so this taco-flavored recipe is a yummy way to use it up! If you omit the meat, it's also a great vegetarian dish.

1 lb. ground beef or turkey
1/3 c. onion, diced
1 c. water
1-1/4 oz. pkg. taco seasoning mix
4 to 5 yellow squash, zucchini or crookneck squash, chopped
1 c. shredded Cheddar cheese

In a skillet over medium heat, brown meat with onion; drain. Stir in water and taco seasoning; add squash. Cover and simmer for about 10 minutes, until squash is tender. Stir in cheese; cover and let stand just until cheese melts. Makes 4 servings.

Quick tip

Serve your favorite skillet supper with a healthy green salad. You have a complete meal with plenty of nutrition.

South-of-the-Border Squash Skillet

Country-Style Skillet Apples

Joanne Nagle, Ashtabula, OH

A perfect partner for roast pork at dinner...for grilled breakfast sausages too!

1/3 c. butter
1/2 c. sugar
1/2 t. cinnamon
2 T. cornstarch
1 c. water
4 Golden Delicious apples, cored, peeled and sliced

Melt butter in a skillet over medium heat. Stir in sugar, cinnamon and cornstarch; mix well and stir in water. Add apple slices. Cook over medium heat, stirring occasionally, until tender, about 10 minutes. Makes 4 to 6 servings.

Ham Steak & Apples Skillet

Gail Blain Peterson, Stockton, KS

My grandmother's old black cast-iron skillet brings back wonderful memories of the delicious things she used to make in it. I seek out scrumptious skillet recipes just so I can use Grandma's old skillet...this one is a real family favorite.

3 T. butter
1/2 c. brown sugar, packed
1 T. Dijon mustard
2 c. apples, cored and diced
2 1-lb. bone-in ham steaks

Melt butter in a large skillet over medium heat. Add brown sugar and mustard; bring to a simmer. Add apples; cover and simmer for 5 minutes. Top apples with ham steaks. Cover with a lid; simmer for about 10 more minutes or until apples are tender. Remove ham to a platter and cut into serving-size pieces. Top ham with apples and sauce. Serves 6.

Country-Style Skillet Apples

Ham Steak & Apples Skillet

Easy Bacon Frittata

Easy Bacon Frittata

Beth Bundy, Long Prairie, MN

Delicious and oh-so-simple to put together! Pair with a fruit salad or a crisp green salad for an easy dinner.

3 T. oil
2 c. frozen shredded hashbrowns
7 eggs, beaten
2 T. milk
12 slices bacon, crisply cooked and crumbled
3/4 c. shredded Cheddar cheese

Heat oil in a large skillet over medium heat. Add hashbrowns and cook for 10 to 15 minutes, stirring often, until golden. In a bowl, whisk together eggs and milk. Pour egg mixture over hashbrowns in skillet; sprinkle with bacon. Cover and reduce heat to low. Cook for 10 minutes, or until eggs are set. Sprinkle with cheese; remove from heat, cover, and let stand about 5 minutes, until cheese is melted. Cut into wedges to serve. Makes 6 servings.

Skillet Goulash

Kari Hodges, Jacksonville, TX

I like to serve up this old-fashioned family favorite with thick slices of freshly baked sweet cornbread topped with pats of butter.

2 lbs. ground beef
10-oz. can diced tomatoes with green chiles
1 lb. redskin potatoes, cut into quarters
15-oz. can tomato sauce
15-1/4 oz. can corn, drained
14-1/2 oz. can ranch-style beans
salt and pepper to taste
Garnish: shredded Cheddar cheese

Brown beef in a Dutch oven over medium heat; drain. Add tomatoes with juice and remaining ingredients except garnish; reduce heat. Cover and simmer until potatoes are tender and mixture has thickened, about 45 minutes. Makes 8 to 10 servings. Garnish with Cheddar cheese.

Sausage Gravy

Leslie Stimel, Columbus, OH

It's a snap to make this delicious homestyle gravy.

1 lb. ground pork breakfast sausage
1/4 c. all-purpose flour
3 to 4 c. milk
1/2 t. salt
1/4 t. pepper

Brown sausage in a large skillet over medium-high heat; do not drain. Stir in flour until mixture becomes thick. Reduce heat to medium-low. Gradually add milk, stirring constantly, until mixture reaches desired thickness. Season with salt and pepper. Serves 4 to 6.

Skillet Goulash

Steak San Marco

Steak San Marco

Darlene Nolen, Whittier, NC

I found this recipe in our local newspaper over twenty years ago. It has become a favorite of our family.

1 lb. beef round steak, sliced into thin strips
1 T. oil
1.35-oz. pkg. onion soup mix
28-oz. can diced tomatoes
3 T. cider vinegar
cooked rice

In a skillet over medium heat, brown beef in oil; drain. Add soup mix to beef; mix well. Stir in tomatoes with juice and vinegar. Bring to a low boil and stir until mixed. Reduce heat; cover and simmer for one hour or until beef is tender, stirring occasionally. Serve over cooked rice. Serves 4 to 6.

Herb & Garlic Shrimp

Cherylann Smith, Efland, NC

This shrimp dish is often requested by my children....and when Daddy isn't looking, they sneak shrimp off his plate!

1 clove garlic, pressed
2 T. olive oil
6 T. butter, sliced
1 lb. fresh shrimp or frozen cooked shrimp, tails on
1.8-oz. pkg. savory herb with garlic soup mix
1 c. warm water

In a skillet over medium heat, sauté garlic in olive oil and butter for 2 minutes. Add shrimp and simmer until shrimp is cooked or thawed, stirring often. Dissolve soup mix in water; pour over shrimp mixture. Reduce heat; simmer until heated through, about 20 minutes. Makes 4 to 6 servings.

Herb & Garlic Shrimp

Pasta à la Drini

Catherine Alesandrini, French Village, MO

This is a great, healthy one-pot meal that's on the table in 30 minutes. It's so versatile...add any herbs or seasonings your family likes.

16-oz. pkg. Italian turkey sausage links
28-oz. can fire-roasted diced tomatoes
1/8 t. red pepper flakes
1/8 t. dried oregano and/or dried basil
10-oz. pkg. frozen chopped broccoli, cooked
16-oz. pkg. whole-wheat penne pasta, cooked

Place sausages on a grill pan over medium heat. Cook until browned and no longer pink in the center; remove from pan and let cool. In a large skillet over medium heat, combine tomatoes with juice and seasonings; bring to a simmer. Slice sausages into bite-size pieces and add to sauce. Add broccoli and pasta to skillet. Return to a simmer and cook for 3 to 5 minutes, until heated through. Serves 4 to 6.

Pasta à la Drini

Huevos Rancheros to Go-Go

Tonya Sheppard, Galveston, TX

All the yummy ingredients are wrapped up in a handy tortilla.

2 c. green tomatillo or red salsa
4 eggs
1/2 c. crumbled queso fresco or shredded Monterey Jack cheese
4 8-inch corn tortillas
Garnish: avocado, sliced

Lightly coat a skillet with non-stick vegetable spray and place over medium heat. Pour salsa into skillet; bring to a simmer. With a spoon, make 4 wells in salsa and crack an egg into each well, taking care not to break the yolks. Reduce heat to low; cover and poach eggs for 3 minutes. Remove skillet from heat and top eggs with cheese. Transfer each egg with a scoop of salsa to a tortilla. Garnish with sliced avocado. Serves 2 to 4.

Pasta Puttanesca

Brandi Joiner, Minot, ND

Such a versatile recipe! It's good either warm or cold.

16-oz. pkg. rotini pasta, uncooked
1 red onion, chopped
1 T. olive oil
5-oz. jar sliced green olives with pimentos, drained
4-oz. can sliced black olives, drained
24-oz. jar marinara sauce
Garnish: grated Parmesan cheese

Cook pasta according to package directions; drain. Meanwhile, in a large skillet over medium heat, sauté onion in olive oil until soft. Add olives; continue to sauté for another 2 to 3 minutes. Add pasta to the skillet and toss to mix. Add marinara sauce; stir well and heat through. Garnish with Parmesan cheese. Serves 6.

Huevos Rancheros to Go-Go

Mom's Best After-Dinner Desserts

(sweet delights)

Weeknight dinners are just a little more special when they end with one of Mom's favorite easy-to-make desserts. Easy-Peasy Berry Cake is filled with oh-so-pretty berries and pairs well with a cup of creamy coffee. Want just a little sweetness after that filling dinner? Try some simple Chocolatey Chewy Brownies or a Pecan Cookie Ball with a hot cup of tea. No matter what sweet goodies you decide to serve, make it easy on yourself with these treat-style recipes that use just 6 ingredients or less!

Chocolate Chip Tea Cookies

Chocolate Chip Tea Cookies

Michelle Sheridan, Upper Arlington, OH

These little cookies look so pretty yet are easy to make.

1 c. butter, softened
1/2 c. powdered sugar
1 t. vanilla extract
2 c. all-purpose flour
1-1/2 c. mini semi-sweet chocolate chips, divided

With an electric mixer on high speed, beat butter and powdered sugar until fluffy. Add vanilla; mix well. Gradually beat in flour; use a spoon to stir in one cup chocolate chips. Form into one-inch balls; place 2 inches apart on ungreased baking sheets. Bake at 350 degrees for 10 to 12 minutes. Remove to wire rack to cool. Place remaining chocolate chips in a small plastic zipping bag. Seal bag; microwave on high until melted, about 30 seconds. Snip off a small corner of bag; drizzle chocolate over cooled cookies. Chill for 5 minutes, or until chocolate is set. Makes about 4 dozen cookies.

Cinnamon-Apple Parfaits

Courtney Robinson, Delaware, OH

A yummy, warm parfait. The baked oat crumble is delicious... try it as an ice cream topping too.

1 c. quick-cooking oats, uncooked
1/2 c. brown sugar, packed
1/4 c. butter, melted
21-oz. can apple pie filling, warmed
1/4 t. cinnamon
1 qt. vanilla ice cream, slightly softened

Combine oats, brown sugar and butter; spread in an ungreased 8"x8" baking pan. Bake at 350 degrees for 10 minutes. Cool; crumble and set aside. Mix together pie filling and cinnamon; divide among 8 parfait glasses. Top with softened ice cream and crumbled oat mixture. Serves 8.

Chocolate-Berry Trifles

Chocolate-Berry Trifles

Melody Taynor, Everett, WA

I've made all kinds of trifles, but this is my first one with chocolate. My sister says it's my best yet!

1 pt. blueberries, divided
1 pt. strawberries, hulled and sliced
1 angel food cake, cubed
1 c. chocolate syrup
12-oz. container frozen whipped topping, thawed

In a bowl, crush 1/4 cup blueberries. Stir in remaining blueberries and strawberries. Place several cake cubes in the bottom of 10 clear serving cups or bowls. Top with a layer of berry mixture. Drizzle lightly with chocolate syrup, then top with a layer of whipped topping. Repeat layers until each cup is full, ending with a layer of whipped topping and a light drizzle of chocolate syrup. Makes 10 servings.

Cherry Dream Pie

Cherry Dream Pie

Clara Buckman, Waverly, KY

Perfect for picnics and potlucks.

8-oz. pkg. cream cheese, softened
1/2 c. powdered sugar
8-oz. container frozen whipped topping, thawed
9-inch graham cracker pie crust
14-1/2 oz. can cherry pie filling

Blend cream cheese and powdered sugar together until smooth and creamy; fold in whipped topping. Spread into pie crust forming a well in the center; fill with pie filling. Chill until firm before serving. Serves 8.

Peach Cobbler Cupcakes

Bonnie Allard, Santa Rosa, CA

My most-requested muffin-like cupcakes...my family & friends love them! They disappear right away whenever I make them to share.

3 c. all-purpose flour
1 c. sugar
1-1/2 T. baking soda
1/2 t. salt
3/4 c. butter, diced
1-3/4 c. milk
15-oz. can sliced peaches, drained and chopped
Optional: brown sugar

Mix flour, sugar, baking soda and salt in a large bowl. Cut in butter with a pastry blender or a fork. Add milk and peaches; stir just until moistened. Spoon batter into 18 greased muffin cups, filling 2/3 full. Add one teaspoon of brown sugar into the center of each cupcake if desired. Bake at 400 degrees for 15 to 20 minutes, until golden. Turn out and cool slightly on a wire rack; serve warm or cooled. Makes 1-1/2 dozen.

Peach Cobbler Cupcakes

Friendship Peppermint Mud Pie

Homemade Vanilla Ice Cream

Jill Valentine, Jackson, TN

2-1/2 c. whipping cream
2 c. half-and-half
2 eggs, beaten
1 c. sugar
1/4 t. salt
2-1/4 t. vanilla extract
Optional: whole strawberries

Combine all ingredients except vanilla in a heavy saucepan over medium-low heat, stirring constantly until mixture is thick enough to coat the back of a spoon and reaches 160 degrees on a candy thermometer. Remove from heat and stir in vanilla. Set pan in an ice-filled bowl; stir. Cover and chill in refrigerator for 8 hours or up to 24 hours. Pour mixture into ice cream maker and freeze according to manufacturer's directions. Garnish with whole strawberries, if desired. Serves 12.

Friendship Peppermint Mud Pie

Lori Vincent, Alpine, UT

Minty chocolate ice cream cake with hot fudge topping...oh my! It doesn't get any better than that!

14-oz. pkg. chocolate sandwich cookies, crushed
  and divided
6 T. butter, melted
1/2 gal. peppermint ice cream, slightly softened
16-oz. jar hot fudge ice cream topping
8-oz. container frozen whipped topping, thawed

Set aside 1/4 cup cookie crumbs. Combine remaining cookie crumbs and melted butter in a large bowl. Toss to coat. Transfer to a greased 13"x9" baking pan; press crumbs firmly to cover bottom of pan. Spread ice cream over crumb crust. Top with fudge topping. Freeze until firm. At serving time, spread whipped topping to edges. Garnish with reserved cookie crumbs. Serves 12.

When I was young, we'd have what we called an "ice cream supper." We would pile in the car and head to the ice cream parlor...that really hit the spot on a hot summer night. —Jill

Homemade Vanilla Ice Cream

Peanut Butter Surprise Cookies

Sherry Gordon, Arlington Heights, IL

Yum, yum, yum! I like to divvy up the dough between baking sheets and chill the second batch while the first is baking.

16-1/2 oz. tube refrigerated peanut butter cookie dough
12 mini peanut butter cups
1/3 c. semi-sweet chocolate chips
1 t. shortening

Divide cookie dough into 12 pieces. With floured fingers, wrap one piece of dough around each peanut butter cup. Place on ungreased baking sheets. Bake at 350 degrees for 10 to 15 minutes, until golden. Cool on baking sheets one minute; remove to wire rack to cool completely. In a saucepan, melt chocolate chips and shortening over low heat, stirring constantly. Drizzle melted chocolate over cookies. Let stand until set. Makes one dozen.

Peanut Butter Surprise Cookies

Pecan Cookie Balls

Jodi Eisenhooth, McVeytown, PA

Make these sweet, crisp little morsels to go with an after-dinner cup of tea or coffee.

1 c. butter, softened
1 c. powdered sugar
2 c. chopped pecans
1 T. vanilla extract
2 c. all-purpose flour
4 T. powdered sugar

Blend together butter and powdered sugar; add pecans, vanilla and flour. Wrap dough in plastic wrap; chill for about 3 hours. Form dough into 3/4-inch balls; place on ungreased baking sheets. Bake at 350 degrees for 10 minutes. Let cool; roll in powdered sugar. Makes 2-1/2 to 3 dozen.

Toffee Almond Treats

Chrissy Stanton, Odenton, MD

So easy to make...so tasty to eat!

1 sleeve saltine crackers
1 c. butter, melted
2 t. vanilla extract
1 c. sugar
12-oz. pkg. semi-sweet chocolate chips
1 c. sliced almonds

Line a baking sheet with aluminum foil; grease. Arrange crackers in a single layer on baking sheet; set aside. Stir together butter, vanilla and sugar in a saucepan; bring to a boil. Spread mixture over crackers; bake at 400 degrees for 4 to 5 minutes. Remove from heat; sprinkle with chocolate chips. Let stand until chips are melted; spread chips over sugar mixture. Sprinkle with almonds; chill for about 2 hours. Break into bite-size pieces. Makes about 2 dozen.

Pecan Cookie Balls

Blue-Ribbon Pecan Pie

Blue-Ribbon Pecan Pie

Gail Kelsey, Phoenix, AZ

This pie has won a blue ribbon at our state fair every time I entered it! It's a family favorite and is always a part of our Christmas dinner.

9-inch pie crust, unbaked
1/2 c. pecan halves
3 eggs
1 c. dark corn syrup
1 c. sugar
1 t. vanilla extract
1/8 t. salt

Place unbaked crust in a 9" pie plate. Arrange pecans in crust; set aside. In a bowl, beat eggs well. Add remaining ingredients; mix well. Pour mixture over pecans in crust. Bake at 400 degrees for 15 minutes; reduce oven to 325 degrees. Bake an additional 30 minutes, or until center of pie is set. Cool completely. Serves 8.

Strawberry Layer Cake

Steven Wilson, Chesterfield, VA

Growing up in North Carolina, spring meant strawberry time, Grandma always baked this delicious cake for the Sunday night church social.

6-oz. pkg. strawberry gelatin mix
1/2 c. hot water
18-1/2 oz. pkg. white cake mix
2 T. all-purpose flour
1 c. strawberries, hulled and chopped
4 eggs
Garnish: fresh strawberries

In a large bowl, dissolve dry gelatin mix in hot water; cool. Add dry cake mix, flour and strawberries; mix well. Add eggs, one at a time, beating slightly after each one. Pour batter into 3 greased 8" round cake pans. Bake at 350 degrees for 20 minutes, or until cake tests done with a toothpick. Cool; assemble layers with frosting. Garnish with strawberries. Serves 12.

Strawberry Frosting:

1/4 c. butter, softened
3-3/4 to 5 c. powdered sugar
1/3 c. strawberries, hulled and finely chopped

Blend butter and powdered sugar together, adding powdered sugar to desired consistency. Add chopped strawberries; blend thoroughly.

Strawberry Layer Cake

Crunchy Biscotti

Crunchy Biscotti

Jo Ann

Afternoon or after dinner, you'll crave these treats with your next cup of coffee. I like to dress up these cookies with a drizzle of white chocolate!

3-1/3 c. all-purpose flour
2-1/2 t. baking powder
1/2 t. salt
1/4 c. oil
1-1/4 c. sugar
2 eggs, beaten
2 egg whites, beaten
Optional: melted white chocolate

Mix flour, baking powder and salt in a large bowl. In a separate bowl, whisk together remaining ingredients except optional chocolate. Blend flour mixture into egg mixture. Divide dough into 3 portions; knead each portion 5 to 6 times, and shape into a ball. Place dough balls on a parchment paper-lined 17"x11" baking sheet. Shape into 9-inch logs; flatten slightly. Bake at 375 degrees for 25 minutes. Remove from oven; place logs on a cutting board. Using a serrated bread knife, cut 1/2-inch thick slices on a slight diagonal. Return slices to baking sheet, cut-side up. Bake for an additional 10 minutes at 375 degrees. Turn slices over; continue baking for 5 to 7 minutes. Let cool and drizzle with white chocolate, if desired; store in an airtight container. Makes about 3 dozen cookies.

Quick tip

An old-fashioned lunch box is a perfect container to fill with homemade goodies and give as a special gift.

Speedy Peanut Butter Cookies

Speedy Peanut Butter Cookies

Tiffany Leiter, Midland, MI

That's correct...there's no flour in these cookies!

1 c. sugar
1 c. creamy peanut butter
1 egg

Blend ingredients together; set aside for 5 minutes. Scoop dough with a small ice cream scoop; place 2 inches apart on ungreased baking sheets. Make a crisscross pattern on top of each cookie using the tines of a fork; bake at 350 degrees for 10 to 12 minutes. Cool on baking sheets for 5 minutes; remove to wire rack to finish cooling. Makes 12 to 15.

Quick & Easy Nutty Cheese Bars

Donnie Carter, Wellington, TX

This recipe is now the requested birthday gift of family & friends. They're so good cold!

18-1/2 oz. pkg. golden butter cake mix
1-1/2 c. chopped pecans or walnuts, divided
3/4 c. butter, melted
2 8-oz. pkgs. cream cheese, softened
1 c. brown sugar, packed

In a bowl, combine dry cake mix, 3/4 cup pecans and melted butter; stir until well blended. Press mixture into the bottom of a greased 13"x9" baking pan. Combine cream cheese and brown sugar in a separate bowl. Stir until well mixed. Spread evenly over crust. Sprinkle with remaining pecans. Bake at 350 degrees for 25 to 30 minutes, until edges are golden and cheese topping is set. Cool completely in pan on wire rack. Cut into bars. Refrigerate leftovers. Makes 2 dozen.

Quick & Easy Nutty Cheese Bars

Easy Cherry Cobbler

Melonie Klosterhoff, Fairbanks, AK

15-oz. can tart red cherries
1 c. all-purpose flour
1-1/4 c. sugar, divided
1 c. milk
2 t. baking powder
1/8 t. salt
1/2 c. butter, melted
Optional: vanilla ice cream or whipped cream

Bring cherries and juice to a boil in a saucepan over medium heat; remove from heat. Mix flour, one cup sugar, milk, baking powder and salt in a medium bowl. Pour butter into 6 one-cup ramekins or into a 2-quart casserole dish; pour flour mixture over butter. Add cherries; do not stir. Sprinkle remaining sugar over top. Bake at 400 degrees for 20 to 30 minutes. Serve warm with ice cream or whipped cream, if desired. Serves 4 to 6.

Quick tip

Serve fruit cobblers with a dusting of powdered sugar instead of whipped cream to save a few calories. It is so pretty and adds that little extra sweetness to enjoy.

Peanut Butter-Chocolate Bars

Eileen Blass, Catawissa, PA

Top with marshmallow creme for s'more fun!

1 c. creamy peanut butter
1/2 c. butter, melted
1 c. graham cracker crumbs
16-oz. pkg. powdered sugar
2 c. semi-sweet chocolate chips, melted

Combine first 4 ingredients together in a large mixing bowl; mix well using a wooden spoon. Press into the bottom of a well-greased 15"x10" jelly-roll pan; pour melted chocolate evenly over crust. Refrigerate for 15 minutes; score into bars but leave in pan. Refrigerate until firm; slice completely through scores and serve cold. Makes 25 to 30.

Coconut Clouds

Charlene Smith, Lombard, IL

For extra sparkle, top with a candied cherry and sprinkle with sugar before baking.

3/4 c. sugar
2-1/2 c. flaked coconut
2 egg whites, beaten
1 t. vanilla extract
1/8 t. salt

Combine ingredients together. Beat with an electric mixer on medium-high speed until soft peaks form. Drop by tablespoonfuls, one inch apart, on a greased baking sheet; bake at 350 degrees for 15 to 20 minutes. Cool on a wire rack. Store in an airtight container. Makes 15 to 20.

Peanut Butter-Chocolate Bars

Mom's Best After-Dinner Desserts

Open-Face Peach Pie

Open-Face Peach Pie

Christy Hughes, Provo, UT

This favorite pie recipe was handed down to me from my grandmother.

1 c. sugar
2 T. cornstarch
9-inch pie crust
6 peaches, peeled, pitted and halved
1 c. whipping cream

Mix sugar and cornstarch together; spread 3/4 of mixture into pie crust. Arrange peaches on top; sprinkle with remaining sugar mixture. Pour cream evenly over peaches; bake at 400 degrees for 10 minutes. Reduce heat to 350 degrees; bake an additional 40 minutes. Makes 8 servings.

Mix-and-Go Chocolate Cookies

Rhonda Reeder, Ellicott City, MD

Just as decadent with peanut butter or milk chocolate chips!

18-1/2 oz. pkg. chocolate cake mix
1/2 c. butter, softened
2 eggs, beaten
1 c. white chocolate chips

In a bowl, combine dry cake mix, butter and eggs until smooth. Mix in chocolate chips. Drop by tablespoonfuls onto ungreased baking sheets. Bake at 350 degrees for 8 to 10 minutes. Let cool on baking sheet for 5 minutes; remove to wire rack to cool completely. Makes about 2 dozen.

Russian Tea Cookies

Lilia Keune, Biloxi, MS

This is an amazing cookie that melts in your mouth. The recipe was given to me by my friend's grandma. It's my go-to recipe when I need something really delicious.

1-1/2 c. butter, softened
1 t. salt
3/4 c. powdered sugar
1 T. vanilla extract
3 c. all-purpose flour
2 c. mini semi-sweet chocolate chips
1/2 c. pecans, finely chopped
Optional: 1/4 c. powdered sugar

In a large bowl, beat together butter, salt, powdered sugar and vanilla. Gradually add flour and mix well. Stir in chocolate chips and pecans. Shape tablespoonfuls of dough into one-inch logs. Place on ungreased baking sheets. Bake at 375 degrees for 12 minutes, or until lightly golden. If desired, sift powdered sugar over hot cookies on baking sheets. Let stand for 10 minutes; remove cookies to wire racks. When cool, immediately store in an airtight container. Makes 4 dozen cookies.

Mix-and-Go Chocolate Cookies

Poppy Seed Cake

Poppy Seed Cake

Holly Curry, Middleburgh, NY

The glaze drizzled over this simple cake sets it apart from other poppy seed cakes.

18-1/4 oz. pkg. yellow cake mix
1 c. oil
1 c. sour cream
1/2 c. sugar
4 eggs, beaten
1/4 c. poppy seed

In a large bowl, beat together dry cake mix and all remaining ingredients. Pour into a greased and floured Bundt® pan. Bake at 325 degrees for one hour, or until a toothpick inserted tests clean. Turn cake out onto a serving plate. Drizzle Glaze over top. Serves 8 to 10.

Glaze:
1/2 c. sugar
1/4 c. orange juice
1/2 t. almond extract
1/2 t. imitation butter flavor
1/2 t. vanilla extract

Combine all ingredients; mix well.

Easy Apple Crisp

Nancy Willis, Farmington Hills, MI

Garnish with a dollop of whipped cream and a dusting of cinnamon or an apple slice.

4 c. apples, cored and sliced
1/2 c. brown sugar, packed
1/2 c. quick-cooking oats, uncooked
1/3 c. all-purpose flour
3/4 t. cinnamon
1/4 c. butter
Garnish: whipped cream, cinnamon, apple slice

Arrange apple slices in a greased 11"x8" baking pan; set aside. Combine remaining ingredients; stir until crumbly and sprinkle over apples. Bake at 350 degrees for 30 to 35 minutes. Garnish as desired. Serves 12 to 14.

Quick tip

Try adding a little lemon yogurt to your whipped topping. The texture is wonderful and the lemon gives the topping a zesty flavor.

Easy Apple Crisp

Chocolate Oatmeal Cookies

Lesleigh Robinson, Brownsville, TN

I've been making these since I was ten years old. They are the simplest cookies I've ever made...you don't even have to bake them!

1/3 c. butter, melted
2 c. sugar
1/2 c. milk
1/3 c. baking cocoa
1/2 c. creamy peanut butter
3 c. quick-cooking oats, uncooked

In a saucepan over medium heat, combine butter, sugar, milk and cocoa. Bring to a boil; cook for one minute. Remove from heat; stir in remaining ingredients. Mix well; drop by rounded teaspoonfuls onto wax paper. Let cookies cool completely. Makes about 2 dozen.

Chocolate Oatmeal Cookies

Easy-Peasy Berry Cake

Peter Kay, Phoenixville, PA

This is the easiest berry cake you can make. It's a great spur-of-the moment dessert and it looks so good, they will think you worked all day on it. Simple ingredients, easy to bake and a great summer dessert! Top it with fresh whipped cream and additional berries for a wonderful dessert, or serve as is with a steaming cup of coffee or tea.

1/2 c. butter, room temperature
3/4 c. plus 1 T. sugar, divided
3 eggs
2 t. baking powder
1 c. plus 1 t. all-purpose flour, divided
1 c. favorite berries, stems removed

In a large bowl, blend butter and 3/4 cup sugar. Add eggs, one at a time, beating after each egg. Add baking powder and one cup flour; stir until smooth. Pour batter into a greased 10" round cake pan or springform pan. Lightly dust berries with remaining flour. Scatter berries over batter and sprinkle with remaining sugar. Bake at 350 degrees for about 40 minutes, testing for doneness with a wooden toothpick. Makes 8 servings.

Honey-Baked Bananas

Amy Greenlee, Carterville, IL

My mom shared this recipe for luscious honeyed bananas.

6 bananas, halved lengthwise
2 T. butter, melted
1/4 c. honey
2 T. lemon juice

Arrange bananas in an ungreased 13"x9" baking pan. Blend remaining ingredients; brush over bananas. Bake, uncovered, at 350 degrees for about 15 minutes, turning occasionally. Serves 6.

Easy-Peasy Berry Cake

Easiest-Ever Cheesecake

Cinnamon Poached Pears

Easiest-Ever Cheesecake

Linda Lewanski, Cosby, TN

You can also drizzle melted chocolate on top for a rich and flavorful twist. Friends will think you spent hours on this simple cheesecake.

12-oz. pkg. vanilla wafers, crushed
1 c. plus 2 T. sugar, divided
1/2 c. butter, melted
2 8-oz. pkgs. cream cheese, softened
12-oz. container frozen whipped topping, thawed
Optional: fresh raspberries

Combine vanilla wafers, 2 tablespoons sugar and butter; press into the bottom of a 13"x9" baking pan. In a separate bowl, blend together remaining sugar and cream cheese; fold in whipped topping. Spread over wafer crust; chill until firm. Garnish with fresh raspberries, if desired. Serves 12 to 15.

Cinnamon Poached Pears

Melanie Lowe, Dover, DE

You'll love this light dessert that's not too sweet.

4 pears
1 c. pear nectar
1 c. water
3/4 c. maple syrup
2 4-inch cinnamon sticks, slightly crushed
4 strips lemon zest

Peel and core pears from the bottom, leaving stems intact. Cut a thin slice off bottom so pears will stand up; set aside. Combine remaining ingredients in a saucepan. Bring to a boil over medium heat, stirring occasionally. Add pears, standing right-side up. Reduce heat and simmer, covered, for 20 to 30 minutes, until tender. Remove pears from pan. Continue to simmer sauce in pan until reduced to 3/4 cup, about 15 minutes. Serve pears drizzled with sauce. Serves 4.

Easy 4-Layer Marshmallow Bars

Jessica Parker, Mulvane, KS

18-1/2 oz. pkg. chocolate cake mix
1/4 c. butter, melted
1/4 c. water
3 c. mini marshmallows
1 c. candy-coated chocolates
1/2 c. peanuts, chopped

Combine cake mix, butter and water until blended; press in a greased 13"x9" baking pan. Bake at 375 degrees for 20 to 22 minutes. Layer marshmallows, chocolates and peanuts over the top. Return to oven for an additional 3 to 5 minutes or until marshmallows melt; let cool. Cut into bars. Makes 2 dozen.

Buttery Lemon Curd

Sandy Roy, Crestwood, KY

An old recipe from England, this lemony spread is irresistible on scones, toast and muffins, even on slices of pound cake!

1 c. butter
2 c. sugar
3 eggs, beaten
1/2 c. lemon juice
1 T. lemon zest

In a double boiler over simmering water, melt butter. Stir in remaining ingredients. Cook, stirring occasionally, for about one hour, or until sauce thickens and reaches 160 degrees on a candy thermometer. Transfer to a covered container; keep refrigerated. Makes 3 cups.

Easy 4-Layer Marshmallow Bars

Marshmallow Graham Custard

Andrea Ford, Montfort, WI

I first made this recipe when I was a little girl. I loved it then and still make it to this day.

1-1/2 c. milk
1/3 c. graham cracker crumbs, finely ground
2 eggs, beaten
2 T. sugar
1/8 t. salt
1/2 t. vanilla extract
8 marshmallows, quartered

In a large bowl, pour milk over cracker crumbs; set aside. In a separate bowl, combine eggs, sugar, salt and vanilla; stir into milk mixture. Stir in marshmallows and pour into 4 ungreased custard cups. Set cups in a shallow pan of hot water. Bake at 325 degrees for 40 minutes, or until a knife inserted in the center comes out clean. Makes 4 servings.

Marshmallow Graham Custard

Chocolatey Chewy Brownies

You'll love these chewy little squares of chocolate!

1 c. butter, softened
2 c. sugar
4 eggs, beaten
1 c. all-purpose flour
4 1-oz. sqs. unsweetened baking chocolate, melted
1 c. chopped walnuts
Optional: powdered sugar

In a bowl, beat butter and sugar with an electric mixer on medium speed, until creamy. Beat in eggs, mixing well. Stir in remaining ingredients. Pour into a greased and floured 13"x9" baking pan. Bake at 350 degrees for 30 minutes. Cool. Dust with powdered sugar if desired. Cut into squares. Makes about 2 dozen.

Raspberry Custard Pie

Sarah Swanson, Noblesville, IN

Our five-year-old daughter collected raspberries every day for a week and wanted to bake a pie. So we made this pie...she and our other kids loved it!

2 eggs, beaten
8-oz. container sour cream
1-1/2 to 2 c. fresh raspberries
1 c. sugar
1 T. all-purpose flour
1/2 t. salt
9-inch pie crust, unbaked

Whisk together eggs and sour cream in a large bowl; set aside. In a separate bowl, combine raspberries, sugar, flour and salt; toss lightly. Add berry mixture to sour cream mixture; mix well and pour into unbaked crust. Bake at 350 degrees for 45 minutes, until firm and golden. Cool completely. Serves 6 to 8.

Chocolatey Chewy Brownies

Berry Crumble

Berry Crumble

Sandy Bernards, Valencia, CA

Instant oatmeal is the key to the scrumptious topping.

4 c. blackberries or blueberries
1 to 2 T. sugar
3 T. butter, softened
3 1-1/2 oz. pkgs. quick-cooking instant oats with maple
   and brown sugar

Toss berries and sugar together in an ungreased 9" pie plate; set aside. Cut butter into quick-cooking oats until coarse crumbs form; sprinkle over berries. Bake at 375 degrees about 30 to 35 minutes until topping is golden. Serves 6.

Creamy Banana Pudding

This creamy pudding will be a family favorite!

5-1/4 oz. pkg. instant vanilla pudding mix
2 c. milk
14-oz. can sweetened condensed milk
12-oz. container frozen whipped topping, thawed
12-oz. pkg. vanilla wafers
4 to 5 bananas, sliced

Combine pudding mix, milks, and topping in a large bowl; mix together until well blended. Spoon one cup of pudding mixture into a large glass serving bowl. Layer with 1/3 each of wafers, banana slices and remaining pudding mixture. Repeat layers twice, ending with pudding mixture. Chill; keep refrigerated.

Plum-Pear Puff Dessert

Joanne Mauseth, Reno, NV

My daughter Amy and I came up with this delicious treat one Sunday afternoon. It is simple, fast and delicious.

1 sheet frozen puff pastry, about 14 by 12 inches
1/4 c. plum jam
1 to 2 pears, cored and sliced
1-1/2 T. brown sugar, packed
1 egg, beaten
1 T. water

Thaw puff pastry at room temperature for about 30 minutes. On a lightly floured surface, roll puff pastry into a 17"x11" rectangle. Lay pastry across a lightly greased baking sheet. Spread jam over half of the pastry, starting on one short edge. Arrange pear slices in a single layer to cover jam; sprinkle with brown sugar. Fold over other half of pastry to cover pears; roll edges to seal. Whisk together egg and water; brush over pastry. With a knife, lightly score pastry to mark desired servings; do not cut through. Bake at 400 degrees for 18 to 20 minutes, until golden. Serve warm or cold. Makes 8 servings.

Strawberry-Rhubarb Pie

Sarah Putnam, Boonville, IN

*I got this recipe from a friend and my whole family loves it...
even my kids who are rather hesitant to try new things!*

1 c. plus 1 T. sugar, divided
1/3 c. all-purpose flour
2 9-inch pie crusts
2 c. strawberries, hulled, sliced and divided
2 c. rhubarb, chopped and divided
2 T. butter, sliced

In a bowl, mix together one cup sugar and flour; set
aside. Line a 9" pie plate with one unbaked crust. Spoon
one cup strawberries and one cup rhubarb into crust.
Sprinkle half of sugar mixture over fruit in crust. Repeat
layers with remaining strawberries, rhubarb and sugar
mixture; dot with butter. Cover with top crust; seal edges
and cut 3 slits in the top to vent. Cover edge of crust with
strips of aluminum foil. Bake at 425 degrees for 40 to
50 minutes, until golden, removing foil 15 minutes before
pie is done. Serves 8.

Strawberry-Rhubarb Pie

White Chocolate Macaroons

Dottie McCraw, Oklahoma City, OK

Ready-made cookie dough makes these super simple.

18-oz. tube refrigerated white chocolate chunk cookie
  dough, room temperature
2-1/4 c. sweetened flaked coconut
2 t. vanilla extract
1/2 t. coconut extract

Combine all ingredients; mix well. Drop by rounded
teaspoonfuls onto ungreased baking sheets; bake at
350 degrees for 10 to 12 minutes. Cool on baking sheets
for 2 minutes; remove to wire rack to cool completely.
Makes 2 dozen cookies.

White Chocolate Macaroons

Chapter 9

Dinner-Friendly Snacks, Treats & Beverages

(goodies to munch and sip)

These quick & easy snacks, treats & beverages are made to be enjoyed before, after or with dinner. Mini Deep-Dish Pizzas can be an appetizer or an entire meal when served with a fresh green salad and a sweet dessert. Switch it up by serving Cherry Tomato Hummus Wraps with a Raspberry Cream Smoothie for a last-minute dinner. Simple Stromboli is so pretty and makes a great snack or simple dinner. So enjoy making these satisfying and tasty bites to enjoy anytime!

Raspberry Punch

Raspberry Punch

Rosie Jones, Wabash, IN

For toasting a festive occasion, replace the cider with sparkling white wine.

2 c. apple cider
3 c. cranberry-raspberry juice cocktail
1 qt. lemonade
Optional: 1 lemon, thinly sliced, fresh raspberries

Combine apple cider, cranberry-raspberry juice and lemonade in a large pitcher or punch bowl. If desired, garnish glasses with lemon slices or raspberries. Makes 8 servings.

Ham & Gruyère Egg Cups

Sonya Labbe, Santa Monica, CA

This recipe is always a favorite and is easy, simple and tasty. It's very pretty too!

12 thin slices deli ham
3/4 c. shredded Gruyère cheese
1 doz. eggs
salt and pepper to taste
1 c. half-and-half
2 T. grated Parmesan cheese

Spray a muffin tin with non-stick vegetable spray. Line each muffin cup with a slice of ham folded in half. Top each ham slice with one tablespoon Gruyère cheese, an egg cracked into the cup, a sprinkle of salt and pepper, one tablespoon half-and-half and 1/2 teaspoon Parmesan cheese. Place muffin tin on a baking sheet. Bake at 450 degrees for 15 minutes, until eggs are set. Allow baked eggs to cool for several minutes before removing them from the muffin tin. Makes one dozen.

Creamy Spinach Dip

Karen Augustson, Frederick, MD

I created this recipe one day for my hungry husband to hold him over until dinner was ready. I've kid-tested this recipe with great success too! Serve with whole-wheat crackers.

10-oz. pkg. frozen chopped spinach, cooked
1/4 c. finely shredded Parmesan cheese
1/4 c. part-skim ricotta cheese
1/4 c. light sour cream
1/4 c. roasted sunflower seed kernels
1/4 t. garlic powder
salt to taste

In a strainer, press spinach to remove as much liquid as possible. Transfer spinach to a bowl. Add remaining ingredients; stir until smooth. If too thick, stir in a little more ricotta cheese to desired consistency. Makes 8 servings, or about 2 cups.

Creamy Spinach Dip

Chicken Ranch Quesadillas

Gretchen Brown, Forest Grove, OR

For an easy-to-handle snack, slice each quesadilla into 8 mini wedges.

1/2 c. ranch dip
8 8-inch flour tortillas
1 c. shredded Cheddar cheese
1 c. shredded Monterey Jack cheese
10-oz. can chicken, drained
1/3 c. bacon bits
Optional: salsa

Spread 2 tablespoons dip on each of 4 tortillas. Top each with one-quarter of the cheeses, chicken and bacon bits. Top with remaining tortillas. Cook each tortilla stack in a lightly greased non-stick skillet or griddle over medium-high heat until lightly golden; turn carefully and cook until cheese is melted. Let stand for 2 minutes; slice into wedges. Serve with salsa, if desired. Serves 4.

Chicken Ranch Quesadillas

Fort Worth Bean Dip

Betty Lou Wright, Hendersonville, TN

When our son moved to Texas, we were introduced to some mighty fine Tex-Mex cooking. I make this tasty dip when he comes home, just so he won't miss all the good eatin' in Fort Worth. Use low-fat products if you like. Serve with nacho tortilla chips...delicious!

15-oz. can refried beans
1 bunch green onions, chopped
1-1/2 c. sour cream
1/2 c. cream cheese, softened
1-1/4 oz. pkg. taco seasoning mix, or to taste
1 c. shredded Cheddar cheese

Combine all ingredients except Cheddar cheese in a lightly greased 2-quart casserole dish. Sprinkle cheese on top. Bake, uncovered, at 300 degrees for 45 minutes, or until hot and bubbly. Makes 12 servings, or about 3 cups.

Cherry Tomato Hummus Wraps

Amber Sutton, Naches, WA

I love those little tomatoes that you can eat like candy straight from the vine! When I added garden-fresh basil and some other salad ingredients I had on hand, I was delightfully surprised with this resulting summer snack.

4 T. hummus
4 8-inch flour tortillas, warmed
1 c. cherry tomatoes, halved
1/2 c. Kalamata olives, chopped
1/3 c. crumbled feta cheese
6 sprigs fresh basil, snipped

Spread one tablespoon hummus down the center of each tortilla. Divide remaining ingredients evenly over hummus. To wrap up tortillas burrito-style, turn tortillas so that fillings are side-to-side. Fold in left and right sides of each tortilla; fold top and bottom edges over the filling. Makes 4 servings.

Cherry Tomato Hummus Wraps

Frosty Orange Juice

Frosty Orange Juice

The orange juice and milk combination in this drink is so refreshing any time of year!

6-oz. container frozen orange juice concentrate,
  partially thawed
1 c. milk
1 c. water
1 t. vanilla extract
1/3 c. sugar
12 ice cubes

Combine all ingredients in a blender container. Cover and blend until frothy. Makes 4 servings.

Mini Deep-Dish Pizzas

Krista Marshall, Fort Wayne, IN

We love deep-dish pizza, but who has time to make it? These delicious bites make a fantastic appetizer, kids' party snack or even a light supper with a green salad on the side.

15-oz. can pizza sauce
1/2 c. grated Parmesan cheese
1 T. Italian seasoning
4 large flour tortillas
1 c. shredded mozzarella cheese
12 slices turkey pepperoni, quartered

In a small bowl, combine pizza sauce, Parmesan cheese and seasoning; stir well and set aside. Spray 12 muffin cups with non-stick vegetable spray. Using a glass tumbler or the empty, rinsed pizza sauce can, cut 3 rounds from each tortilla. Rounds should be just a little larger than muffin cups. Gently press tortilla rounds into muffin cups, covering each cup on the bottom and up the sides a little. Spoon 2 tablespoons sauce mixture into each cup; sprinkle with mozzarella cheese. Top each cup with 4 pieces pepperoni. Bake at 400 degrees for 10 to 15 minutes, until golden and crisp. Let stand 2 minutes; remove from muffin tin with a fork. Serve warm. Makes 6 servings of 2 mini pizzas each.

Quick tip

Try grating fresh cheese for your pizzas and salads. You'll love the fresh taste and it only takes a minute to do!

Mini Deep-Dish Pizzas

Cheesy Spinach-Stuffed Mushrooms

Cheesy Spinach-Stuffed Mushrooms

Cinde Shields, Issaquah, WA

10-oz. pkg. frozen chopped spinach, thawed and
   squeezed dry
1/4 c. cream cheese, softened
1 c. crumbled feta cheese
3/4 t. garlic powder
1/4 t. pepper
24 mushrooms, stems removed
1 c. grated Parmesan cheese

In a bowl, combine all ingredients except mushroom
caps and Parmesan cheese; mix well. Spoon mixture into
mushrooms; place on a rimmed baking sheet. Sprinkle
mushrooms with Parmesan cheese. Bake at 350 degrees
for 15 to 20 minutes, until bubbly and heated through.
Serve warm. Makes about 8 servings.

*These warm, savory, bite-size
beauties always seem to find their
way onto my holiday appetizer
menu. In fact, I love these
mushrooms so much that I even
serve them to my family for dinner
year 'round with a side of quinoa
and a hearty salad. -Cinde*

Stuffed Cherry Tomatoes

Betty Reeves, Cardington, OH

*These appetizers are a real hit at family picnics, especially
with homegrown cherry tomatoes just ripened and picked off
the vine. They are so easy to make and simply delicious.*

1 lb. bacon, crisply cooked and crumbled
24 cherry tomatoes
1/2 c. mayonnaise
1/2 c. green onion, finely chopped
2 T. fresh parsley, chopped
salt and pepper to taste

Set aside prepared bacon on paper towels to drain. Cut
a thin slice off the top of each tomato; discard slices.
Use a small spoon to hollow out tomatoes; discard pulp.
Combine remaining ingredients in a bowl; blend well.
Spoon mixture into hollowed-out tomatoes. Refrigerate
until chilled. Makes 2 dozen.

Hot Crab Spread

Kara Allison, Dublin, OH

*If you like seafood, you'll really go for this creamy, crabby
spread.*

2 8-oz. pkgs. cream cheese, softened
16-oz. can refrigerated pasteurized crabmeat, drained
   and flaked
2 T. green onion, finely chopped
1/2 c. prepared horseradish
1/2 c. sliced almonds
paprika to taste

Beat cream cheese until smooth; blend in crabmeat,
onion and horseradish. Spread in an ungreased one-
quart casserole dish. Top with almonds and sprinkle with
paprika. Bake, uncovered, at 375 degrees for 20 minutes.
Makes about 4 cups.

Cheesy Potato Puffs

Barb Sulser, Columbus, OH

We can't stop nibbling on these golden morsels!

4-oz. pkg. instant potato flakes
1/2 c. shredded Cheddar cheese
1/2 c. bacon bits
Optional: paprika

Prepare potato flakes according to package directions; let cool. Stir in cheese; roll into 1-1/2 inch balls. Roll balls in bacon bits; arrange on an ungreased baking sheet. Sprinkle with paprika, if desired. Bake at 375 degrees for 15 to 18 minutes. Serves 4.

Cheesy Potato Puffs

Simple Stromboli

Diane Williams, Mountain Top, PA

1 green pepper, thinly sliced
1 onion, thinly sliced
1 T. butter
13.8-oz. tube refrigerated pizza crust
1/2 lb. deli ham or roast beef, thinly sliced
8 slices mozzarella cheese
pepper to taste

In a skillet over medium heat, sauté green pepper and onion in butter until tender. Unroll unbaked pizza crust on a lightly greased baking sheet. Layer crust with slices of meat and cheese; top with green pepper mixture and season with pepper. Roll crust loosely into a tube, jelly-roll style; pinch top and sides closed. Bake, seam-side down, at 375 degrees for about 25 minutes, until golden. Slice to serve. Serves 4.

Jo Ann's Holiday Brie

Jo Ann

One of my favorite recipes...great for "pop-in" guests.

13.2-oz. pkg. Brie cheese
1/4 c. caramel ice cream topping
1/2 c. sweetened dried cranberries
1/2 c. dried apricots, chopped
1/2 c. chopped pecans
1 loaf crusty French bread, sliced, toasted and buttered

Place cheese on an ungreased microwave-safe serving plate; microwave on high setting for 10 to 15 seconds. Cut out a wedge to see if center is soft. If center is still firm, return to microwave for another 5 to 10 seconds, until cheese is soft and spreadable. Watch carefully, as center will begin to melt quickly. Drizzle with caramel topping; sprinkle with fruit and nuts. Serve with toasted slices of crusty French bread. Makes 6 to 8 servings.

Simple Stromboli

Chicken-Salsa Dip

Chicken-Salsa Dip

Margaret Collins, Clarendon Hills, IL

This recipe becomes dinner when I add a fresh fruit salad and some cookies and ice cream for dessert!

8-oz. jar salsa, divided
8-oz. pkg. cream cheese, softened
8-oz. pkg. shredded Mexican-blend cheese
2 to 3 boneless, skinless chicken breasts, cooked
  and diced

Blend half the salsa with the cream cheese; spread on the bottom of an ungreased 9" pie pan. Top with remaining salsa; sprinkle with cheese and chicken. Bake at 350 degrees for 25 minutes. Serves 8.

Pepperoni Pizza Bites

Bacon Quesadillas

Edward Kielar, Whitehouse, OH

These savory snacks have zing...what flavor!

1 c. shredded Colby Jack cheese
1/4 c. bacon bits
1/4 c. green onion, thinly sliced
Optional: 4-1/2 oz. can green chiles
Optional: 1/4 c. red or green pepper, chopped
4 6-inch flour tortillas
Garnish: sour cream, salsa

Combine cheese, bacon bits and onion in a small bowl; add chiles and peppers, if desired. Sprinkle mixture equally over one half of each tortilla. Fold tortillas in half; press lightly to seal edges. Arrange on a lightly greased baking sheet. Bake at 400 degrees for 8 to 10 minutes until edges are lightly golden. Top with a dollop of sour cream and salsa. Serves 4.

Pepperoni Pizza Bites

Nancy Kremkus, Ann Arbor, MI

Get creative and try this recipe with alternative toppings...you'll have a blast! So fun to make with the kids.

11-oz. tube refrigerated thin pizza crust
1/2 c. pizza sauce
8 slices pepperoni
1/2 c. shredded mozzarella cheese

Do not unroll pizza crust; cut into 8 equal pieces. Arrange dough 3 inches apart on parchment-lined baking sheet. Flatten each piece of dough into a 2" circle. Spoon pizza sauce into each center. Top each pizza with pepperoni and cheese. Bake at 400 degrees for 12 minutes or until golden and cheese melts. Makes 8 mini pizzas.

Chinese Chicken Wings

Chinese Chicken Wings

Trisha Donley, Pinedale, WY

This recipe can also be made with chicken drummies. Serve them with ranch dressing for dipping and celery stalks for a cool crunch. This is a very easy recipe, a quick go-to that's so yummy.

1/2 c. soy sauce
1/2 c. brown sugar, packed
1/2 c. butter
1/4 c. water
1/2 t. dry mustard
4 lbs. chicken wings

Combine all ingredients except wings in a saucepan; cook for 5 minutes over medium heat. Place wings on an ungreased large shallow baking pan; brush with sauce. Bake at 350 degrees for one hour, turning occasionally and brushing with remaining sauce. Makes about 20 wings.

Witchy's Chickpea Wraps

Anne Tassé, Orillia, Ontario

I added my own little bit of magic to a simple hummus-type spread and wrapped it in tortillas! These roll-ups are so easy to make, and you can add your own little touches. They're one of the first things to go at all of my gatherings.

19-oz. can garbanzo beans, drained and rinsed
1/2 c. fresh parsley or dill, chopped
2 to 4 cloves garlic, minced
juice of 1 lemon
1/2 c. olive oil
5 to 6 10-inch flour tortillas, any flavor
Optional: lemon wedges

Combine all ingredients except tortillas and lemon wedges in a food processor or blender. Process to a smooth paste, adding a little more olive oil if needed. On each tortilla, spread about 2 tablespoons of mixture out to the edge. Roll up tightly; place tortillas seam-side down on an ungreased baking sheet. Bake at 350 degrees for about 15 to 20 minutes, until edges are lightly crisp. Slice each tortilla into one-inch pieces. Serve with lemon wedges, if desired. Makes 8 servings of 3 pieces each, or 2 dozen.

Raspberry Cheese Ball

Julie Ann Perkins, Anderson, IN

Try different preserves to accommodate everyone's tastes... cherry, apricot or even boysenberry!

2 8-oz pkgs. cream cheese, softened
1/4 c. raspberry preserves
2 c. pecans, finely chopped and divided
assorted cookies and crackers

In a bowl, beat cream cheese until creamy; mix in preserves and one cup pecans. Shape into a ball and roll in remaining pecans. Serve with cookies and crackers. Serves 6 to 8.

Ricotta Gnocchi

Eleanor Dionne, Beverly, MA

This is my mother's recipe from more than forty years ago. She made all her pasta by hand. My children look forward to these each time I make it. Now my daughter has learned how to make these and my grandchildren can't wait to eat them. Very easy to do!

32-oz. container ricotta cheese
1 egg, beaten
1 t. salt
4 c. all-purpose flour, divided
Garnish: tomato sauce, grated Parmesan cheese

Combine ricotta, egg and salt in a large bowl; mix thoroughly with a large spoon. Gradually add flour, one cup at a time. When dough is no longer sticky, knead slightly on a lightly floured board. Break off chunks; roll into long ropes. Cut ropes into pieces the size of a cherry. Roll in a little flour with the back of a fork. Place on a clean tea towel to dry. To serve gnocchi, boil for 8 to 10 minutes in a large pot of salted water. Garnish with warmed tomato sauce and Parmesan cheese. Serves 6.

Smoky Sausage Wraps

Vickie McMonigal, Altoona, PA

Serve these little pigs-in-a-blanket with spicy brown mustard for dipping.

16-oz. pkg. cheese-filled cocktail sausages
3 T. barbecue sauce
1 T. maple syrup
8-oz. tube refrigerated crescent rolls
Garnish: additional barbecue sauce

Place 32 sausages in a medium saucepan; reserve any remaining sausages for another recipe. Stir in barbecue sauce and maple syrup. Cook over medium heat until heated through; let cool for 5 to 10 minutes. Separate crescents into triangles; cut each triangle into 4 long, thin triangles. Wrap one triangle of dough around each sausage; pinch ends to seal. Arrange on an ungreased baking sheet. Bake at 350 degrees until golden. Serve with additional sauce for dipping. Makes 32 wraps.

Ricotta Gnocchi

Raspberry Cream Smoothies

Raspberry Cream Smoothies

Shirl Parsons, Cape Carteret, NC

I have been making these refreshing smoothies for years. They're a delicious treat for any time of day!

3 c. frozen raspberries
1 c. banana, cubed and frozen
2 c. orange juice
2 c. frozen vanilla yogurt
2 c. raspberry yogurt
2 t. vanilla extract

In a blender, combine frozen fruit and remaining ingredients. Process until smooth; stir, if needed. Pour into chilled glasses. Makes 8 servings.

Cappuccino Cooler

Dianne Gregory, Sheridan, AR

A perfect beverage to serve after dinner!

1-1/2 c. brewed coffee, cooled
1-1/2 c. chocolate ice cream, softened
1/4 c. chocolate syrup
crushed ice
Garnish: frozen whipped topping, thawed
Optional: chocolate-covered espresso beans

Blend coffee, ice cream and syrup together until smooth; set aside. Fill 4 glasses 3/4 full with crushed ice; pour in coffee mixture. Top each with a dollop of whipped topping and an espresso bean, if desired. Serve immediately. Makes 4 servings.

Honey-Glazed Snack Mix

Cindy Elliott, Modesto, IL

A perfect snack to munch while doing homework! This recipe is from my friend, Mary Beth Mitchell. I like the taste of this best when I use fresh honey from the farmers' market or orchard.

5 c. corn and rice cereal
3 c. mini pretzel twists
2 c. pecan halves
1/2 c. honey
1/2 c. butter, melted

Combine cereal, pretzels and pecans in a large bowl; set aside. Blend together honey and butter. Pour over cereal mixture; toss to coat. Spread on ungreased baking sheets. Bake at 300 degrees for 10 minutes. Stir and continue to bake an additional 10 to 15 minutes. Pour onto wax paper and cool completely. Store in airtight containers. Makes about 10 cups.

Honey-Glazed Snack Mix

Rocky Mountain Cereal Bars

Karen Ensign, Providence, UT

These homemade snack bars will disappear quickly!

2/3 c. sugar
2/3 c. corn syrup
1 c. creamy peanut butter
6 c. doughnut-shaped multi-grain oat cereal
3/4 to 1 c. sweetened dried cranberries

Combine sugar, corn syrup and peanut butter in a large saucepan over low heat. Stirring mixture constantly, heat through until peanut butter is melted. Remove from heat. Add cereal and dried cranberries; mix well. Spread cereal mixture evenly into a lightly greased 13"x9" baking pan. Cool completely; cut into bars. Makes about 2-1/2 dozen bars.

Rocky Mountain Cereal Bars

Brie Kisses

Kathy Grashoff, Fort Wayne, IN

Delicate and pretty cheesy bites that you'll love serving.

2/3-lb. Brie cheese, cut into 1/2-inch cubes
17.3-oz. pkg. frozen puff pastry
1/3 c. red or green hot pepper jelly

Arrange cheese cubes on a plate and place in the freezer. Let pastry thaw at room temperature for 30 minutes. Unfold each sheet of pastry and roll with a rolling pin to remove creases. Slice each sheet into quarters; slice each quarter in half. Slice each piece in half one more time for a total of 32 squares. Place squares into greased mini muffin cups; arrange so corners of dough point upwards. Bake at 400 degrees for 5 minutes. Place one cheese cube in center of each pastry. Bake an additional 10 minutes, until edges are golden. Remove pastries from tin; immediately top each with 1/2 teaspoon jelly. Serve warm. Makes 2-1/2 dozen.

Brie Kisses

Parmesan Dill Dressing & Dip

Wendy Ball, Battle Creek, MI

I like to make our mealtimes special with lots of homemade items, both for everyday and for holidays. This salad dressing is easy to make and stores very well in the refrigerator. Enjoy it as a salad dressing or a dip for your favorite fresh veggies.

1-1/2 c. mayonnaise
3/4 to 1 c. shredded Parmesan cheese
3 T. dill weed
2 T. whipping cream or milk
3 cloves garlic, chopped
1 t. pepper
1/2 t. onion powder

Blend all ingredients in a bowl. Cover and refrigerate until serving time. If serving as a vegetable dip, arrange assorted vegetables around bowl. If using as a salad dressing, thin with cream or milk to pouring consistency.

Creamy BLT Dip

Barbara Thurman, Carlyle, IL

Put the "L" in BLT! Simply spoon dip into a hollowed-out head of lettuce for serving.

1 lb. bacon, crisply cooked and crumbled
1 c. mayonnaise
1 c. sour cream
2 tomatoes, chopped
Optional: chopped fresh chives, chopped tomatoes

Blend together bacon, mayonnaise and sour cream; chill. Stir in tomatoes just before serving; sprinkle with chives or chopped tomatoes, if desired. Makes 2-1/2 cups.

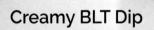
Creamy BLT Dip

Cinnamon-Sugar Crisp Strips

Cinnamon-Sugar Crisp Strips

Melissa Fraser, Valencia, CA

Once you taste these, you'll have trouble walking away from more. Try dipping them in warm cinnamon-apple pie filling. When my mother taught me to make this recipe, we used wonton wrappers. I modified it slightly and now use flour tortillas, but both taste great.

1 T. cinnamon
1 c. sugar
oil for deep frying
8 10-inch flour tortillas, cut into 1-inch strips

Combine cinnamon and sugar in a bowl; set aside. Heat 2 inches of oil in a heavy skillet over medium-high heat. Add 5 to 7 tortilla strips at a time; cook for 20 to 40 seconds on each side until crisp. Drain on a paper towel-lined plate for 5 minutes, then sprinkle with cinnamon-sugar mixture. Place strips and remaining cinnamon-sugar mixture into a paper bag. Gently toss tortilla strips to coat well. Remove from bag and arrange on a serving plate. Serves 6 to 8.

Monkey Bread

Michelle Pettit, Sebree, KY

This scrumptious dish is always a big hit. I usually have to make two batches because someone will always try to sneak away with one to take home!

1/2 c. sugar
1-1/2 t. cinnamon
3 12-oz. tubes refrigerated biscuits, quartered
1 c. brown sugar, packed
1/2 c. butter, melted
2 T. water

Combine sugar and cinnamon in a bowl. Roll biscuit pieces in sugar mixture; place in a greased Bundt® pan. Combine brown sugar, butter and water; pour over biscuits. Bake at 350 degrees for 30 minutes. Invert onto a serving plate. Serves 6 to 8.

English Cider

This warm and spicy drink is yummy any time of year, but especially when winter is in the air!

1/2 c. brown sugar, packed
1-1/2 qt. apple cider
1 t. whole allspice
2 cinnamon sticks
2 t. whole cloves
1 orange, sliced and seeded

Combine ingredients in a large stockpot. Spices can be placed in a tea strainer, if preferred, or added loose. Cover and simmer for 25 minutes. Strain before serving if necessary. Makes 6 to 8 servings.

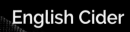

English Cider

Index

Breads & Crackers

Blue Cheese Cut-Out Crackers, 179
Busy-Day Banana Bread, 170
Cheddar-Dill Bread, 158
Cream Cheese Crescent Rolls, 166
Crispy Corn Fritters, 172
Delicious Quick Rolls, 152
Homemade Bagels, 47
Kathy's Bacon Popovers, 168
Kelly's Easy Caramel Rolls, 151
Mile-High Buttermilk Biscuits, 176
Monkey Bread, 296
Soft Sesame Bread Sticks, 148
Swope Bread, 160

Cakes, Cookies & Bars

Chocolate Chip Tea Cookies, 251
Chocolate Oatmeal Cookies, 268
Chocolatey Chewy Brownies, 272
Coconut Clouds, 263
Crunchy Biscotti, 261
Easy 4-Layer Marshmallow Bars, 271
Easy-Peasy Berry Cake, 268
Lemon-Poppy Seed Cake, 109
Mix-and-Go Chocolate Cookies, 264
Peach Cobbler Cupcakes, 253
Peanut Butter-Chocolate Bars, 263
Peanut Butter Surprise Cookies, 256

Pecan Cookie Balls, 256
Poppy Seed Cake, 266
Quick & Easy Nutty Cheese
   Bars, 262
Rocky Mountain Cereal Bars, 293
Russian Tea Cookies, 264
Speedy Peanut Butter Cookies, 261
Strawberry Layer Cake, 258
Toffee Almond Treats, 256
White Chocolate Macaroons, 275

Desserts

Berry Crumble, 274
Blue-Ribbon Pecan Pie, 258
Buttery Lemon Curd, 271
Cherry Dream Pie, 253
Chocolate-Berry Trifles, 251
Cinnamon-Apple Parfaits, 251
Cinnamon Poached Pears, 270
Creamy Banana Pudding, 274
Easiest-Ever Cheesecake, 270
Easy Apple Crisp, 266
Easy Cherry Cobbler, 262
Friendship Peppermint Mud Pie, 254
Homemade Vanilla Ice Cream, 254
Honey-Baked Bananas, 268
Marshmallow Graham Custard, 272
Open-Face Peach Pie, 264

Peachy Good Dessert, 109
Plum-Pear Puff Dessert, 274
Raspberry Custard Pie, 272
Strawberry-Rhubarb Pie, 275
Tahitian Rice Pudding, 109

Mains/ Beef

5-Can Mexican Meal, 20
Anita's Onion Steaks, 230
Beef & Noodle Skillet, 222
Beef Porcupine Meatballs, 222
Broccoli Beef Stir-Fry, 235
Cheeseburger Bake, 205
Chicago Italian Beef, 79
Corned Beef Casserole, 186
Daddy's Shepherd's Pie, 199
Easy Slow-Cooker Steak, 87
Family Favorite Chili Mac, 224
Glazed Corned Beef, 98
Ground Beef & Kale Curry, 235
Hunter's Pie, 184
Linda's Rigatoni Bake, 194
Make-Ahead Faux Lasagna, 27
Mashed Potato Pie, 190
Meatball-Stuffed Shells, 206
Mom's Meatloaf, 17
Mom's Spaghetti & Meatballs, 24
Muffin Tin Meatloaves, 10
My Mom's Stuffed Peppers, 188
Nana's Easy Pot Roast, 96

Index

Newlywed Beef & Noodles, 96

Pepperoni-Pizza Rigatoni, 93

Poor Man's Steak & Vegetables, 203

Quick & Easy Lasagna, 206

Quick Meatballs, 20

Savory Herb Roast, 90

Simple Baked Mostaccioli, 37

Skillet Goulash, 242

Slow-Cooker Swiss Steak, 82

South-of-the-Border Squash
   Skillet, 238

Steak San Marco, 244

Swiss Steak, 90

Tamale Pie, 208

Tom's Easy Meatloaf, 27

Mains/ Chicken & Turkey

Apple-Stuffed Turkey Breast, 84

Buttermilk Fried Chicken, 224

Chicken & Rice Casserole, 217

Chicken Artichoke Pasta, 105

Chicken Spaghetti, 232

Company Chicken & Stuffing, 80

Curried Chicken with Mango, 235

Easiest-Ever Turkey Dinner, 106

Easy-As-1-2-3 Chicken Bake, 206

Easy Chicken Pot Pie, 214

Fruity Baked Chicken, 31

Garlic Parmesan Chicken, 10

Jennifer's Soy Sauce Chicken, 14

Joan's Chicken Stuffing
   Casserole, 87

Lemon Wine Chicken Skillet, 220

Lemony "Baked" Chicken, 94

Mexicali Chicken Stack-Ups, 188

Mom's Cola Chicken, 222

Mustard Chicken, 208

One-Pan Roast Chicken Dinner, 184

Overnight Scalloped Turkey, 34

Pasta à la Drini, 246

Poppy Seed Chicken, 80

Santa Fe Chicken & Potatoes, 236

Slow-Cooker Chicken Cacciatore, 76

Slow-Cooker Country Chicken &
   Dumplings, 98

Spicy Chicken Casserole, 214

Tammy's Italian Chicken, 83

Tempting Teriyaki Chicken, 238

Zesty Picante Chicken, 102

Mains/Fish & Seafood

Crab & Broccoli Rolls, 158

Herb & Garlic Shrimp, 244

Tuna Seashell Salad, 179

Mains/Pork

Apple Spice Country Ribs, 76

Apricot-Glazed Ham Steaks, 23

Baked Pork Medallions, 18

Breezy Brunch Skillet, 232

Country Pork Skillet, 232

County Fair Italian Sausages, 98

Crock O' Brats, 84

Easy Bacon Frittata, 242

Egg Casserole Deluxe, 213

Ham Frittata, 228

Ham Steak & Apples Skillet, 240

Lazy Pierogie Casserole, 101

Maple Pork Chops, 29

Melt-in-Your-Mouth Pork Chops, 88

Mimi's Stuffed Pork Chops, 200

Parmesan Baked Pork Chops, 33

Penne Sausage Bake, 194

Peppered Pork Loin, 24

Pork Chops à la Orange, 101

Pork Chops Ole, 230

Saucy Pork Chops, 190

Index

Sausage Gravy, 242
Skillet Apples & Pork Chops, 230
Slow-Cooked Pulled Pork, 82
Slow-Cooker Ham & Broccoli
    Meal-in-One, 76
Slow-Cooker Sauerkraut Pork
    Roast, 106
Smoky Hobo Dinner, 94
Spicy Sausage & Rice, 236
Tangy Pork Ribs, 90
Yummy Pork Ribs, 206

Mains/Egg, Vegetable & Grains

Angie's Pasta & Sauce, 139
Baked Garden Omelet, 130
Blueberry Pillows, 119
Broccoli Quiche Peppers, 139
California Omelet, 112
Cheddar Baked Spaghetti, 196
Cheese & Chive Scrambled
    Eggs, 115
Cheese & Onion Pie, 188
Chile Relleno Casserole, 196
Cowboy Macaroni & Cheese, 184
Creamy Fettuccine Alfredo, 140
Dad's Famous French Toast, 142
Denver Oven Omelet, 217
Eggs Benedict, 134
Festive Brunch Frittata, 226

French Onion Tart, 116
French Toast Casserole, 213
Golden Macaroni & Cheese, 200
Goldenrod Eggs, 115
Grandma McKindley's Waffles, 134
Herbed Mushroom Omelets, 126
Huevos Rancheros to Go-Go, 246
Inside-Out Stuffed Pepper, 220
Johnny Appleseed Toast, 122
Light & Fluffy Pancakes, 35
Lizzy's Make-Ahead Egg
    Casserole, 38
Melinda's Veggie Stir-Fry, 130
Mexican Egg Bake, 119
Mom's Macaroni & Cheese, 137
Mom's Sweet Apple Omelet, 112
Olive & Feta Cheese Omelet, 236
Pasta Puttanesca, 246
Peanut Butter French Toast, 142
Rosemary Peppers & Fusilli, 228
Salsa Lasagna, 13
Sassy Spaghetti Sauce, 37
Savory Italian Pancakes, 122
Scott's Wonderful Waffles, 132
Spicy Black Bean Scrambled
    Eggs, 126
Spinach & Tomato French Toast, 142
Summer Squash Pie, 203
Tasty Spaghetti Sauce, 20

Tasty Tortilla Stack Pie, 137
Texas Toads in the Hole, 133
Tortino de Carciofi, 121
Uncle Dave's Oven Pancakes, 133

Pizzas

Buffalo Chicken Pizza, 17
Egg-Topped Pizza, 119
Garden-Fresh Pesto Pizza, 124
Kristin's Perfect Pizza Dough, 12
Mini Deep-Dish Pizzas, 282
Pepperoni Pizza Bites, 289
Poppy's Onion Pizza, 140

Quiches

Beef & Cheddar Quiche, 210
Hashbrown Quiche, 186
No-Crust Spinach Quiche, 115
Pepperoni & Cheese Quiche, 38
Quick & Easy Quiche, 199

Salads & Dressings

Apple-Walnut Chicken Salad, 167
Bacon-y Romaine Salad, 164
Bowtie Salad with Tomatoes &
    Zucchini, 180
Caprese Salad, 155
Chicken-Broccoli Rotini Salad, 155
Chilled Apple & Cheese Salad, 166
Chunky Tomato-Avocado Salad, 157

Index

Confetti Corn & Rice Salad, 180
Crabby Tuna Salad, 165
Crisp Celery-Pear Salad, 174
Dilly Cucumber Salad, 174
Fresh Kale Salad, 157
Grandmother's Red-Hot Salad, 14
Granny's Macaroni Salad, 31
Greek Orzo Salad, 176
Green Goddess Bacon Salad, 148
Heavenly Rice, 170
Island Chicken Salad, 152
Jolene's Chickpea Medley, 116
Lemon-Herb Chicken Salad, 160
Lucy's Sausage Salad, 164
Mama's Cucumber Salad, 151
Marinated Broccoli Salad, 168
Pea Salad, 166
Penne & Goat Cheese Salad, 172
Ryan's Yummy Pasta Salad, 155
Sesame-Asparagus Salad, 162
Shrimp & Orzo Salad, 165
Summer Spinach Salad, 158
Sweet Ambrosia Salad, 162

Sandwiches & Burgers

Avocado Egg Salad Sandwiches, 42
Baby PB&J Bagel Sandwiches, 59
Bacon Quesadillas, 289
BBQ Chicken Calzones, 52
Caesar Focaccia Sandwich, 64
California Pita Sandwiches, 42
Cherry Tomato Hummus Wraps, 280
Chicken Ranch Quesadillas, 280
Creamy Tuna Sandwiches, 50
Dad's Wimpy Burgers, 54
Easy Sloppy Joes, 54
Egg Salad Sandwiches, 61
Excellent Burgers, 57
Extra-Cheesy Grilled Cheese, 68
Favorite Egg Muffins, 62
French Bread Pizza Burgers, 72
Garlic & Mustard Burgers, 57
Grilled Havarti Sandwiches, 44
Grilled Panini, 59
Herb Garden Sandwiches, 67
Hot Chicken Slow-Cooker
    Sandwiches, 96
Irene's Portabella Burgers, 124
Kathy's Denver Sandwich, 47
Louisiana Sausage Sandwiches, 48
Marty's Special Burgers, 50
Mini Ham & Cheesewiches, 45
Monster Meatball Sandwiches, 67
Peanut Butter Apple-Bacon
    Sandwich, 70
Pepper Steak Sammies, 64
Ranch BLT Wraps, 70
Raspberry-Dijon Baguettes, 51
Rise & Shine Sandwiches, 62
Scott's Ham & Pear Sandwiches, 64
Skinny Salsa Joes, 72
So-Good Turkey Burgers, 47
Strawberry Patch Sandwich, 132
Sweet Smoky Sandwiches, 67
Suzanne's Tomato Melt, 129
Tangy Turkey Salad Croissants, 48
Tex-Mex Burgers, 42
Toasted Green Tomato
    Sandwiches, 68
Texas Steak Sandwiches, 61
Trail Mix Bagels, 132
Triple-Take Grilled Cheese, 52
Wanda's Wimpies, 61
Weeknight Treat Burgers, 57
Yummy Ham Sandwiches, 94

Side Dishes

Broccoli Supreme, 205
Cheesy Chile Rice, 210
Corn Surprise, 121
Country Cabin Potatoes, 79
Country-Style Skillet Apples, 240
Creamy Italian Noodles, 134
Family-Favorite Corn Souffle, 192
Fried Pecan Okra, 145

Index

Fried Spaghetti, 121

Grandma Dumeney's Baked Beans, 18

Green Bean Baked Lucette, 217

Green Bean Saute, 57

Hashbrown Casserole, 208

Homemade Soup Noodles, 22

Homestyle Butterbeans, 51

Minted Baby Carrots, 45

Mom's Cheesy Hashbrowns, 190

Parmesan Scalloped Potatoes, 186

Roasted Tomato-Feta Broccoli, 226

Savory Rice Casserole, 214

Simmered Autumn Applesauce, 109

Simple Scalloped Tomatoes, 129

Simple Skillet Peaches, 228

Spicy Sweet Potato Fries, 59

Summertime Tomato Tart, 112

Tamara's Pickled Beets, 23

Texas Hominy, 192

Vidalia Onion Side Dish, 145

White Cheddar-Cauliflower Casserole, 199

Soups & Stews

Chili-Weather Chili, 16

Dan's Broccoli & Cheese Soup, 87

Down-Home Split Pea Soup, 106

Easy Slow-Cooker Beef Stew, 79

Elizabeth's Slow-Cooker White Chili, 102

Lisa's Chicken Tortilla Soup, 28

Make-Ahead Tomato Soup, 33

Mexican Chicken Chili, 93

Slow-Cooker Beefy Taco Soup, 105

Slow-Cooker Butternut Squash Soup. 80

Slow-Cooker Rich Beef Stew, 101

Slow-Cooker Smoked Sausage Stew, 102

Stuffed Pepper Soup, 24

Snacks, Appetizers, Dips & Beverages

Brie Kisses, 294

Cappuccino Cooler, 292

Cheesy Potato Puffs, 286

Cheesy Spinach-Stuffed Mushrooms, 285

Chicken-Salsa Dip, 289

Chinese Chicken Wings, 290

Cinnamon-Sugar Crisp Strips, 296

Creamy BLT Dip, 294

Creamy Spinach Dip, 278

English Cider, 296

Fort Worth Bean Dip, 280

Fresh Herb Pesto Sauce, 13

Frosty Orange Juice, 282

Ham & Gruyère Egg Cups, 278

Honey-Glazed Snack Mix, 293

Hot Crab Spread, 285

Jo Ann's Holiday Brie, 286

Mom's Slow-Cooker Mini Reubens, 88

Parmesan Dill Dressing & Dip, 294

Raspberry Cheese Ball, 290

Raspberry Cream Smoothies, 292

Raspberry Punch, 278

Ricotta Gnocchi, 291

Simple Stromboli, 286

Smoky Sausage Wraps, 291

Stuffed Cherry Tomatoes, 285

Witchy's Chickpea Wraps, 290

Send us your favorite recipe

and the memory that makes it special for you!*

If we select your recipe for a brand-new **Gooseberry Patch** cookbook, your name will appear right along with it...and you'll receive a FREE copy of the book!

**Submit your recipe on our website at
www.gooseberrypatch.com/sharearecipe**

*Please include the number of servings and all other necessary information.

Have a taste for more?

Visit www.gooseberrypatch.com to join our Circle of Friends!

- Free recipes, tips and ideas plus a complete cookbook index
- Get special email offers and our monthly eLetter delivered to your inbox

You'll also love these cookbooks from Gooseberry Patch!

150 Backyard Cookout Recipes

150 Best-Ever Cast Iron Skillet Recipes

Our Favorite Bacon Recipes

Our Favorite 30-Minute Meals

Easy Classic Casseroles

Comfort Food Lightened Up

Slow Cooker to the Rescue

Cook it Quick

Secrets from Grandma's Kitchen

Church Potluck Favorites

Fun Fall Foods

Christmas Comfort Classics

www.gooseberrypatch.com